"Engaging and enthusiastic, Jason Brubaker has written an excellent introduction to the new landscape of filmmaking - especially for those just starting out their careers."

Jon Reiss, author of "Think Outside The Box Office"
www.JonReiss.com

"There are lots of books that tell you the technical aspects of how to make a movie. This one answers the question you'll face when it's done: 'Now what?' If you care about having people actually pay to see your movie, get this book."

Jurgen Wolff, author of "Your Writing Coach"
www.ScreenwritingSuccess.com

"Jason Brubaker's 'Filmmaking Stuff' gives the Independent Filmmaker a rare insight into how to make a feature film with a proven step-by-step formula from an indie filmmaker who has 'been-there-done-that-and got the T-shirt.' Not only does Jason Brubaker understand the business and creative side of filmmaking, he is also an expert in using the Internet and Social Media to finance and distribute any film today. This fact alone is reason enough to always have this book sitting beside your computer."

Peter D. Marshall, Filmmaker
www.ActionCutPrint.com

"Jason personally guides you through the many important things you need to know to create a great film. This book has exceptional tips for saving money and marketing."

Carole Dean, author of "Art of Funding Second Edition"
www.FromTheHeartProductions.com

"A real page turner. This is a must read for any filmmaker who does not enjoy being suckered by middlemen."

Kim Callahan, Hollywood Talent Manager

"Speaking from his own hard won experience, Jason lays out a comprehensive plan to help the modern indie filmmaker get films made. If you care more about making good movies and telling good stories, than about being Hollywood, let Filmmaking Stuff show you the way."

Gordon Firemark, Entertainment Attorney
www.firemark.com

"The process of script to distribution is now much more complicated and labor intensive. Producers must wear even more hats on the job and be much more knowledgeable about the business of film than they once were. Fortunately, Jason has written this book to help educate and inspire producers of this new century to take advantage of the wonderful tools the internet has given us all to reach audiences worldwide."

Sheri Candler, Marketing and Publicity Specialist
www.shericandler.com

"If you want to make movies, if you already make movies and want to sell them, if you already sell movies and want to make more money, you owe yourself a few hours with Jason's newest book. It has the potential to change everything for you. I don't know anyone who knows (and appreciates) indie DIY filmmaking better than Jason. 'Filmmaking Stuff' is packed with solid knowhow; it's that one serious tool that indies have been needing."

Norman C. Berns, Producer/Director
www.reelgrok.com

Jason Brubaker's Filmmaking STUFF

How to Make, Market and Sell your Movie Without the Middleman

copyright 2012 Brubaker Unlimited LLC
www.filmmakingstuff.com

Copyright © 2012, Jason Brubaker, All rights reserved.

Published by: Brubaker Unlimited LLC 6767 Sunset Boulevard, #153 Los Angeles, California 90028

Take Action: Make Your Movie Now! ® is a registered trademark of Brubaker Unlimited LLC and may not be used without written permission from the author. Visit www.FilmmakingStuff.com for more information and filmmaking resources.

Author's Note: This book is based heavily on the author's filmmaking experience. When possible, he has included personal examples. With that said, you may have a question or two, so feel free to email the author at: Jason@FilmmakingStuff.com

Warning – Disclaimers: This book is designed to provide information on modern moviemaking and filmmaking. It is sold with the understanding that the author or publisher is not providing tax, accounting, legal, investment, business or other professional advice. Filmmaking is risky. While the process of making movies can be fun, filmmaking can also be detrimental to your life, wellbeing and savings account. The information in this book is meant to supplement, not replace, proper filmmaking training. Like any business involving money, employees, personal and professional liability and emotions, Filmmaking poses inherent risks. Although the author and publisher have made every effort to ensure that the information in this book was correct at press time, the information contained herein is limited. This book is meant to provide a viewpoint on filmmaking and serve as a supplement to other texts and information on the subject. The purpose of this book is to educate and entertain. The author and publisher do not assume and hereby disclaim any liability to any party for any loss, damage, or disruption caused by errors or omissions, whether such errors or omissions result from negligence, accident, or any other cause. Many of the companies, products and services mentioned in this book are affiliates of Brubaker Unlimited LLC. This means that the publisher gets paid to recommend various products and services. Your price will not be affected. Please conduct your own due-diligence prior to making ANY purchases both here and everywhere on earth. Before making any business or financial or life decision, you are advised to speak with the necessary qualified tax, legal and business professionals.

No part of this book may be reproduced or transmitted in any form or by any means without written permission of the author. Filmmaking is a risky business.

Cover design by Ian Hannin - www.IanHannin.com
Book editing by Noel Lloyd
Back cover photo of Jason Brubaker by Charity Read

ISBN-13: 978-1475076189

Printed in the United States of America

Dedicated to my Mom and Dad

Filmmaking Success Mindset

What I think about becomes real.

I play to my strengths. I support my weak areas with talented collaborators.

I take advice from people with experience.

I spend time with people who make me feel better about myself. I work to make others feel good too.

Following dreams is easier with money in the bank. I save what I can and avoid debt.

I keep an idea book and write down movie ideas as they come my way.

My word is trust. I never break my word.

I deserve filmmaking success because I am creative and passionate.

I always bring my ideas to fruition.

Table of Contents

Introduction 15

Chapter One 21

    Set Your Goals 22

    Manage Time 23

    Save FU Money 25

    Stop Asking Permission 28

    The Backyard Indie 30

    Create Your Company 33

    Establish Your Movie Website 34

    Reserve Your Domain 34

    Website Platform 35

    Your Company Website 36

    Movie Ideas 37

    Build Your Team 39

    Test Your Team 41

    Make Short Movies First 42

    Keep Your Day Job 43

Chapter Two 45

Research Your Concept 46

Target Your Market... 47

Pick Your Story 48

Screenwriting... 49

Make a Movie Poster 51

Create a Movie Website.. 52

Start Blogging 53

Build Your Audience List... 55

Social Media for Modern Moviemakers 58

Facebook... 60

Tweet This 62

Create a YouTube Channel 63

Get LinkedIn 64

Movie Work Is Reality.. 65

Chapter Three.. 67

Scheduling and Budgeting Software...................................... 69

Define the Scale 70

Get Legal Help... 71

How Do I Get the Money?	73
Develop Your Personal Brand	75
Your Circle of Influence	76
Manage Your Reputation	77
Network without Becoming a Jerk	78
Build Unforgettable Rapport	79
Meet Rich People	81
Hollywood Money 101	82
Establish Income	84
Earned Income	84
Passive Income	84
Residual Income	85
Portfolio Income	85
Business Plan	86
Crunch the Numbers	87
Video on Demand for Rent	88
Direct DVD Sales	89
Small Business Filmmaking	91
Crowdfunding	92

Another Way to Get Money 94

Chapter Four 97

    Create a Plan B 99

    Get Legal Releases 100

    Find a Director 100

    Attaching Actors 101

    Auditions 102

    The Table Read 103

    The Director of Photography 103

    Audio 104

    Photos on Set 105

    Get Crew 105

    Food Is Finance 106

    Lock Your Locations 107

    Befriend the Press 108

    Production 110

    Get Some Sleep 111

    Wrap Party 113

    Edit Your Movie 114

Get Music 116

After Your Vacation 117

Chapter Five 119

Film Festival Marketing.. 120

Sharpen Your Hook 122

The VOD Aggregator... 124

Enter the Marketplace.. 125

Create Your Movie Sales Funnel 127

Refine Your Trailer and Promote It 130

Increase Web Traffic... 132

Press Releases.. 134

Online Advertising.. 135

Pay-Per-Click.. 135

Cost-Per-Impression 136

Offline Print Advertising.. 137

Monitor Visitor Data 138

    Time on Site 138

    Keyword Phrases.. 138

    Traffic Sources 139

Social Bookmarking for Your Movie 139

Leverage Your Following 141

Find Other Filmmakers 142

Modern Moviemaking Manifesto 145

Resources 147

Movie Making Checklist 149

Sell Your Movie Checklist 157

How to Create a Press Kit 161

Acknowledgements 163

About The Author 165

Introduction

Long before I made a single penny making movies, I was stuck in my small town, living with my parents. To make ends meet, I took a job selling dishwashers and garbage disposals. Back then, I was like a lot of people. I knew I wanted to make movies, but I really had no idea how to get started. In fact, I felt discouraged, depressed and lost.

Like most independent filmmakers, I was inspired by the news of Kevin Smith, Ed Burns and the other indie filmmakers who were finding innovative ways to get movies made, seen and sold. These guys inspired me to take action and gain experience. I remember reading everything I could get my hands on about the filmmaking process, hoping to find a step-by-step system that would show me how to make a movie and then sell it for a gazillion dollars. I had to take action!

After saving all summer to buy a used Arri BL 16mm camera and a few rolls of film, I spent an entire weekend producing my movie. After buying beer for the wrap party, I promptly ran out of money. So for the next six months, I worked to save enough money to process the film and transfer it to video. I remember coming home each night and gazing lovingly at three 400-foot rolls of exposed 16mm film collecting dust on my bedroom floor. My movie was called "Oh Baby." It was a silly movie. But this was proof that I was indeed a filmmaker.

While I did eventually get the movie processed, transferred to video, and edited – I couldn't help but feel a little disheartened. I mean, if it took me a year just to finish a short film, how long would it take to get a feature made? To answer this question, I moved to New York City, where I ended up working alongside a (then) 20-something year old entrepreneurial producer, Seth Carmichael. With Seth, I learned what it took to make features.

But I also found out about the next major hurdle to filmmaking success: discriminatory distribution.

During that time, I remember sitting in on meetings with prospective investors. Most were experienced business professionals from other industries who immediately understood that even the best indie movie was worthless without distribution.

The fact that independent filmmakers could not access distribution meant that it would tough to reach an audience. And without an audience, there would be no sales. This fact alone made it very tough to raise money. But even with the odds stacked against us - like most filmmakers, we believed that if we could just make the movie, the money would come.

"I'm going to make my movie and sell it at Sundance!"

Back then, the Sundance Dream was so intoxicating that most filmmakers refused to acknowledge that that only a handful of independent movies actually got accepted into the festival. And most of those movies failed to garner a distribution deal that actually paid. Still, this did not stop filmmakers from trying.

Heck, even when a rejection letter from Sundance arrived in the mail, many of these feature filmmakers still blindly clung to the hope that things would turn out well. I mean, there was always the possibility of getting noticed at a secondary film festival. But after a few months on the regional festival circuit, with no sign of a distribution deal, many of these once enthusiastic filmmakers gave up hope and went back to their day jobs.

I am speaking from experience. After leaving New York I moved to Los Angeles. I decided it was time to test my luck at winning the Sundance Dream. I knew the odds of garnering a profitable distribution deal were against us. So to increase our chances of success, we decided to dump our limited resources into a niche audience focused, silly zombie movie. While the movie was not Oscar caliber, it did have a remarkable hook that promoted word of mouth buzz. As a result, we received quite a few calls from prospective distributors and sales agents.

We were excited! But instead of writing us a check, many of these guys simply expected us to relinquish our movie rights for the mere validation of seeing our zombie movie at local video stores. *"We won't make money, but we can rent our movie."*

I knew the odds of getting a gazillion-dollar check were improbable. And just like the filmmakers that came before us, we held out hope that someone would discover us and give us some money. But it never happened.

Luckily, we did have one last strategy: We decided to try selling our movie on the internet, through Amazon. Now I want to make something clear. This was a time when the idea of selling movies over the internet was new. And nobody liked the idea is because the concept of self-distribution was considered derogatory. So you can imagine our surprise when we made over a few thousand dollars over a few short months!

This experience forever changed the way I viewed filmmaking.

Before we go further, you need to know something. If you are reading these words, looking for more information on three-point lighting or how to set up dolly track, you are in the wrong place. While all of that technical stuff is essential, you can find this information in just about every filmmaking book ever published. And you probably already have a bookshelf full of that stuff.

In this book, you will discover strategies on how to leverage popular movie marketplaces like iTunes, Amazon and Hulu for maximum profit. You will also learn how to run your filmmaking as a serious business.

Everything you're about to absorb represents insights I discovered only through trial, error, frustration and sleepless nights. The methods I reveal may seem at times unconventional. But if you keep an open mind, you might gain one tip (or a dozen) that will immediately improve the way you view filmmaking.

Also, since the average American lives for only 27,010 days, time is running out. Your life is too short to waste. What are you waiting for? NOW is time to make, market and sell your movie! If you are willing to roll the dice and make your movie, then you have an obligation to yourself, your cast and crew to make the best, most successful independent movie ever. And you do not need my permission. If you want to write, you write. If you want to direct, you direct. If you want to make your movie this year, do it!

But before you jump in, it helps to know what you want. Some filmmakers want recognition. Others want a pile of money. And other people simply want a nice title on a business card and a little respect. Regardless of your desired career outcome, you need to determine the price you're willing to pay to achieve your success. What are you willing to sacrifice in terms of effort, time, money and frustration to make movies?

As you move toward the realization of your filmmaking goals, I would like to tell you there is no such thing as luck. But I can't. Some people always seem to be a little further ahead of the majority. These are the top 20 percenters. And to the outside world, these lucky go-getters seem unstoppable. But when asked to reveal their secrets for success, many of these lucky people would share stories of hard work and endless rejection.

I learned how to create luck when I was in college. To raise money to finance my student film, I took a job selling expensive hot tubs at a local carnival. I was given an incentive: Sell two hot tubs per carnival, and, in addition to my commission, I would also receive a $500 bonus. Because I needed the money, I was driven to pitch hot tubs to every person who walked within 10 feet of me, including college kids, grandmothers, fathers, mothers and children with ice cream melting down their hands…It didn't matter. The only way to make money was to get the sales.

Most people rejected me outright. Other folks listened to my entire pitch before they rejected me. And the vast majority of folks asked to "think it over" and never returned. After running the numbers, I realized that out of every 100 people I got rejected 98 times. But I also made two sales. This taught me a simple lesson. I realized that if I wanted something in life, I just had to ask enough people. Years later, it dawned on me that raising money for movies was the same as selling hot tubs. The more people you pitch, the luckier you get.

While I am on the subject of luck, there are a lot of people who get into the movie business who have never experienced rejection. These are people with lots of enthusiasm, but no defined plans for success. As a result, most of these folks get shot down after a few attempts. They pack their bags and hop on the first bus back to wherever they came from. Your job is to become tougher than the majority. Recognize rejection as part of the process. And if you aren't getting rejected daily, you're not trying hard enough. Rejection is the universe asking you how badly you want success.

There has never been a better time to make, market, and sell movies. For $2,000, filmmakers can grab a camera, shoot a feature, and compete for virtual "shelf space" in iTunes, Amazon, Hulu and most every other movie marketplace.

There is one thing you must remember: While all of this innovation is exciting, filmmakers must now plan their filmmaking business from inception to distribution. As a result, your success comes down to these focused questions:

1. Who is your target audience?
2. How large is your target audience?
3. How will you reach your target audience?
4. What is the marketing cost to achieve this?
5. How many unit sales will it take to break even?

These are questions you will answer in detail during the business-planning process for your movie. In the event you choose not to answer these questions, then you know from day one that your odds of success are decreased. Without a defined market or an established sales channel, it is difficult to justify financing. This makes it a challenge to pay cast and crew, which can derail your dreams of producing a movie.

Assuming you are willing to face this new world, you are in the right place. In the following pages, I am going to share some strategies on how to answer these questions.

If you are ready to push forward, take action, and make your movie now, then I only have one question for you:

Given the resources that you have right now, what is the movie that you can make this year?

Chapter One

Modern Movie Business

"If you want to be successful, find someone who has achieved the results you want and copy what they do and you'll achieve the same results."

–Tony Robbins

What is your definition of success?

Achieving success requires dedication, hard work and even some luck. And if you don't establish a grounded perspective and plan, the pursuit of a movie career will most certainly make friends and family think you're self-absorbed, egotistical and a little crazy. And if you don't make time for these important people, they may be correct!

The movie industry is full of great opportunities. But if you don't believe these opportunities exist, or if you don't believe you deserve greatness, you'll never experience coolness. So before you make your dreams real, you must first visualize the life you want. Once you have a clear image of what this looks like, your ideal life is yours if you are willing to pay the price.

If you want to write, you write. If you want to direct, you direct. If you want to make a movie, you do it. And if you want to waste your Hollywood years impressing phonies at parties, you can do that too. The successful people in the movie business know what they want. They put blinders on. They focus, and they go for it. Everything these people do is in line with their driving desire to succeed. Heavyweights don't waste time with people or activities that distract them from their goals.

Set Your Goals

If you're going to survive the sleepless nights of the movie world, you really need to understand who you are and what you want. I know this is cliché, but it's true. Nobody will respect you until you respect yourself. If you come to Hollywood without having the confidence to be genuine, you'll get swept into the mix, lose focus, and wonder why you failed.

If you haven't already done so, you need to write down a few goals. The process is very simple, and the results will be profound. Without clear and concise WRITTEN goals, it will take you much longer to achieve success. Talk to any Hollywood Heavyweight, and you will find that having clear goals is tantamount to accomplishment.

How tough is your skin? I say this because you'll need to assess your ability to overcome rejection. There are a lot of people who come to Hollywood with a vision, yet who have never experienced rejection. Do not become one of these people. Whenever you are faced with rejection, you must always remember everyone has a messed-up sense of reality. The person rejecting you could be stupid or perhaps they just are not interested in you at this time. Great. Fail fast and move on!

Seriously. There is nothing you can do about other people. In fact, some people are so stupid that they project their lack of originality and creativity onto the world. What they reject in you isn't you, it's them. It means nothing, really. Your job is to recognize rejection as a filter mechanism and as part of getting what you want. When you go after something BIG, if you aren't getting rejected daily, you're not playing hard enough.

While attempting to land my first production gig, I got rejected daily. People told me that without experience it would be hard for me to get a job. But that did not stop me. To gain experience, I started volunteering to work for free on some local productions. This enabled me to get the necessary experience to push forward towards my next goals. Remember, everybody starts somewhere. And the person willing to be told "no" many times also gets told "yes" many times as well.

Manage Time

Everything you do in life revolves around time. When you start planning your movie productions, your time will become the most valuable asset you have. Your ability to manage time could mean the difference between success and failure. According to Hollywood standards, failure is spending 10 years in this town with nothing to show for it. Don't be one of those people.

In your quest to move into the inner circle of Hollywood, you will encounter so many distractions that it will make your head spin. When you get out here, you'll quickly notice that this town offers some of finest nightlife in the world. Be prepared to spend nights sampling the tasty beverages of the Sunset Strip.

There is nothing wrong with this, but between doing some sort of demanding job to pay rent and trying to go to the grocery store, you will soon realize time flies. Unless you become proficient at time management, you could go years without a movie. And if you are not in the habit yet, you will want to start using some kind of daily planner or a time management application on your phone. In my only business, I am pretty simple. I use the task manager in my Gmail, as well as my Google calendar. However, there are many options out there.

If you're serious about your success, you'll need to start planning your life in half-hour increments. For many, this might seem too rigid or too much of a pain in the ass. But if you can discipline yourself to do this, you'll soon realize that you'll accomplish much more in six months than other people will accomplish in two years. Resolve today to start planning your time right down to the half hour, and you'll quickly realize how much time you've been wasting.

You need to prioritize. What exactly does it mean to prioritize? It means breaking down your BIG goals into manageable chunks and then writing them down every morning. Once you have your goals written out, combine them with the more mundane tasks of living, such as doing laundry.

Once your goals are written down, prioritize with letters. For my list, I utilize the classic ABC method. I write an A next to everything that needs to be done first. Everything else gets a B or C. Most of the time, activities that get you closer to your ideal life are a priority. For example, if you are 20 days away from producing a film, and you don't have a location yet, getting a location is your priority.

However, sometimes paying rent is your priority. Without paying the rent, you don't have a place to live. And without that place to live, making a movie is secondary. Unless,of course, you don't mind sleeping in your car. In that case, who the heck cares about rent?

A typical list would look like this:

- ☐ Write for one hour.
- ☐ Call producer for meeting.
- ☐ Update Quicken Online.
- ☐ Laundry
- ☐ Go surfing.

What is priority is determined by you. For today, "laundry" is my most important priority. I have a meeting with a producer tomorrow, and I need clean socks and underwear. Without clean socks and underwear, I would risk smelling like a pig, and nobody (aside from pig farmers) wants to work with a pig. On other days, updating my banking might be the priority. This is because money is essential. And if I'm taking a producer out to lunch, I'll need to know how much money I have in my bank account to make sure I have enough to cover the meal and avoid any embarrassment.

Once you prioritize habitually, you will race ahead of the pack. The vast majority of people who want a career making movies waste their days. They live life thinking in terms of "someday." Someday they will make a movie. Someday they will budget their time. Someday they will make a phone call.

Someday, life will end.

When you know your goals, and you make a habit of breaking your BIG goals into small, daily tasks based on priority, you become power player.

Every goal you attempt to achieve teaches you something new about yourself and helps you grow. There is really no such thing as failure. There is only experience. And every experience helps you refine a skill. During the course of your career, it's possible you'll start out with one goal in mind and end up somewhere entirely different. This is part of the process. With every skill you gain, you grow as a person.

Save FU Money

If you want to make movies, get out of debt and save up some FU money. What is FU money? It's the money you've saved that allows you to eventually take a few months off from your day job so you can find investors and possibly put together a movie deal. In other words, with FU money in the bank, it is far easier to take calculated risks that may result in the successful realization of your movie dreams. But when you have a ton of debt, you may find yourself at a severe disadvantage.

My first credit card purchase was in college. I used plastic to pay rent for a semester. I also purchased a Star Wars poster from one of those late-night shopping channels. Then I bought a pizza and a case of beer. Next thing you know, a decade flies by, and I found myself carrying a revolving $5,000 balance. Sometimes I got lucky and paid down my balance. Once, I even paid my credit card off in full. But like a failed diet, after a couple months, I found myself right smack back where I was before—and sometimes I was worse off. Why?

Lucky for me, I had some friends who were credit card debt free. After talking with them, I soon realized people get into debt for the following reasons:

1. People spend more than they make.
2. People identify themselves as people in debt.

After giving my debt addiction considerable thought, I realized my external debt was actually a reflection of my internal beliefs about money. In other words, somewhere in my mind, I identified myself as someone in debt. This was reflected in my everyday conversations about money. I would say things like: "I have debt." Or, "I'm in debt." Or, "I have $5,000 in debt." Talking like this only served to reinforce my debt-burdened identity. As a result, I continued to swipe plastic over and over.

Your peer group will influence your success in life. Take a look at your closest friends and I bet they have the same amount of debt as you. Mine did. But after moving to Hollywood, I dated a woman who made a lot less money than me, yet she lived debt free. Hanging out with her changed my beliefs about money and debt. I started to think debt was unacceptable! I realized I too could live debt free. I stopped using my credit cards and began a recovery plan.

It may take you a week or 10 years, but if you want to make movies, you need to eradicate your credit card debt. To achieve this, you must first change your words, which will change your thoughts, which will change your beliefs, which will eventually change your actions, which will subsequently change your bank balance!

Here are my personal debt reduction tidbits:

1. Hang out with people who are debt free.
2. Freeze your credit card in a block of ice.
3. Pretend as if you already live debt free.

In addition to the above action steps, starting TODAY, even if it sounds like a lot of BS, repeat the following mantra every morning until you believe your words:

1. I have lots of money saved up.
2. Using credit cards kills my dreams.
3. I pay myself first!

Remember, the faster you break your credit card addiction, the faster you free yourself up to make movies. So if you forget everything else I mention — remember the following words:

QUIT USING YOUR CREDIT CARD!

In this way, at least you won't continually make your debt worse. And once you break the cycle of using your credit card, you can start shifting your strategy toward debt repayment and, eventually, the accumulation of FU money. The best part is that you can get started today.

Stop Asking Permission

In the movie business, power is measured by your ability to get a movie made. That's it. Most people don't have the power to make movies. In fact, most people only have the power to say, "NO!" And if you're a filmmaker working to make your first feature, you've probably heard:

"NO! We don't accept unsolicited submissions."

"NO! We do not work with first-time filmmakers."

"NO! We don't think there is any upside to your project."

"NO! We will not fund your movie."

But you know what? I hate asking permission to make movies. Asking permission makes me feel like a little kid. Truly independent filmmakers make movies regardless of what anyone says. Most importantly, powerful people never ask for permission to create their world. It's true. When powerful people want to accomplish something, they do it. So if you want to be powerful, you need to stop asking permission and just go after everything you want. Of course, this is easier said than done.

Let me put this into perspective. I'd like you to pretend you are similar to me and that you really love frozen yogurt. And let us also pretend that instead of becoming a successful filmmaker, you dream of opening up your own yogurt shop.

Would you wait around for someone to give you permission to open a frozen yogurt shop? I hope not.

Then why are you waiting for Hollywood to give you permission to make your movie? Powerful people never ask: "Will you read my screenplay?" They say: "I'm producing a feature next year and looking for collaborators." This is the secret to success. Your success is determined by your ability to ask for the things you want in life. If you don't ask, you don't get.

Get it?

When I worked for an independent producer in New York City, I participated in various movie pitch meetings with prospective investors. Those meetings usually went something like this: "We've got a great screenplay, and we would like you to invest." And invariably, the typical response was: "Great! How will you return my investment?" It was at this point that we would describe our Sundance Dream strategy. *"If we are lucky, we will get into Sundance and make a gazillion dollars."*

Back then, if you were fortunate enough to actually get a movie made, your next step involved getting into film festivals and crossing your fingers that an acquisitions executive would give you a paycheck. If you were super lucky, you would go on to make your three-picture deal. This was the era of the Sundance Dream. And as many filmmakers found out, there is a big difference between a dream and a solid business plan.

When you compare the independent film business to other businesses, there are quite a few similarities. Think about it. Factory owners establish brick-and-mortar companies to produce a product. As a filmmaker, you hire a cast and crew to produce your movie. But despite these differences, both the factory owner and the filmmaker manufacture products ready for the marketplace. And this is where things get a little wacky.

Unlike the factory owner who has access to his or her own marketing, sales and distribution channels, filmmakers have traditionally relied on the blessings of third-party movie distribution companies in order to access the movie marketplace. And for many filmmakers, taking a crappy deal offered by one of these discriminatory distributors was better than nothing.

Given the fact that most video stores are now on the demise, the idea of giving away your rights simply to get onto the shelves of a local video store seems silly. But back then, you could not access any marketplace without asking permission. Given these restraints, it is no wonder why most prospective investors balked at the idea of putting money into movies.

Luckily, over the past decade everything about filmmaking has gotten awesomely better. Equal access to popular Internet marketplaces now allows every filmmaker the freedom to make, market and sell their movies without the middleman. While this does not guarantee all filmmakers will produce great cinema, it does mean that filmmakers can finally create a mini-studio movie business with very little resistance.

The Backyard Indie

If you are a filmmaker with ambition and a dream, you should not hesitate. You should not wait for Hollywood to give you permission to make your movie - but rather, you should grab a camera and Make Your Movie Now!

Welcome to the world of Backyard Indies.

Backyard indie filmmakers are no longer prohibited by cash or creativity. Yet despite this reality, many of my high profile "professional" friends in Los Angeles have made a conscious effort to pretend that inexpensive HDSLR filmmaking doesn't count as real filmmaking! When referencing these movies, common questions asked by Hollywood hotshots are: Who signed the SAG agreements? Who contacted the unions? Who notified the MPAA so that movie will be rated? Who gave you permission to call this a "real" feature film?

Nobody.

Guess what? A prospective customer seeking a movie on iTunes does not care if your movie was an official union indie or a backyard indie made for pocket change. And thanks to the demise of traditional distribution and the increased market domination of iTunes, Amazon and other VOD outlets, the big difference between a $10,000 backyard indie and a $2 million "real" indie is no longer determined by the budget. What determines the success of any movie is who gets the most clicks on his or her "BUY NOW" button.

But before you get too excited – know this: Getting movies seen and sold is very challenging. Simple math reveals that the filmmaker who needs to recoup $2 million is going to need a lot of web traffic and a TON of sales!

In this example, to recoup $2 million, the filmmaker will need to sell (roughly) 200,000 video on demand downloads at $10 a pop. And because most marketplaces charge around 40 percent for the privilege of setting up shop, these first sales will cover the costs allocated to VOD service providers (the real winners here); after which, the filmmaker will still need to sell an additional 200,000 downloads to recoup the initial investment.

> 400,000 VOD downloads x $10 = $4,000,000
> MINUS $2,000,000 in VOD fees = The initial $2,000,000

Meanwhile, the filmmaker with who opted to create a $10K backyard indie only has to sell 2,000 VOD downloads to recover the initial costs. And if the backyard indie was crowdfunded (I will explain crowdfunding in a later chapter) and the movie gets buzz, and the stars align, the filmmaker may have an awesome release and potentially profit on day one. But this is not guaranteed. The only thing that is guaranteed is that the less money you spend on the movie equals the less money you need to recoup when it comes time to sell your movie.

While nobody wants to make movies for pocket change, many filmmakers still believe they can somehow continually produce unprofitable (movie) products and still expect the money and the subsequent production jobs supported by the investment of Other People's Money (OPM) to keep rolling in. This is unsustainable and just bad business. Unlike in the old days, filmmakers can no longer approach prospective investors with the cliché pitch: *"Filmmaking is a risky investment — if we are lucky, we might win Sundance and get a deal."*

Now, with non-discriminatory distribution options available to all filmmakers, that line of give-me-money reasoning is reckless, no longer applicable, and, in my opinion, unethical.

Aside from the initial challenge of sales and marketing, the ripple effect reveals a greater conundrum: How will you raise enough money to pay your cast and crew, while at the same time keep your costs low enough so that you can sell the necessary units needed to recoup your initial investment?

To survive the volatility of indie filmmaking, you will need both a short-term game and a long-term game. Short term, you will obviously want to make a movie. Long term, because the market is saturated with many backyard indies, you will need to start thinking of yourself as a mini-studio, continually focused on building your brand and sourcing your own audience. To achieve this, you will need plan for creating multiple titles over time, resulting in a very genre-specific movie library.

While creating a mini-studio may seem beyond the scope and scale of what you think is possible, setting your sights high is much more proactive than ignoring the fact that Backyard Indies are now competing for the same virtual shelf space as mainstream Hollywood movies. We are in a time of change. This is the indie movie distribution equivalent of the automobile replacing the horse-drawn wagon. Seize this opportunity!

The time is quickly approaching when all entertainment will be on-demand and very inexpensive to consume. It comes down to this: Will you ignore this movement and continue to cross your fingers, hoping some middle-man will grant you a dream distribution deal? Or will you start sourcing your audience?

Create Your Company

Before you start pitching your project too heavily, and especially before you speak with any prospective investors regarding your movie project, you should first speak with a qualified professional on ways you can protect yourself from business liability. Now, I'm not a lawyer. And the rules of business vary depending on where you live. So you will need to speak with a qualified professional in your own state or country. But the basic rule is this: Divide your personal life from your business!

As a filmmaker, the moment you start planning your project, you are in business. It is at this point that many filmmakers create a business card and set up a website touting the wonders of their projects. It is also at this point when many costly mistakes are made. The ways in which you establish and conduct your filmmaking business can have legal and tax ramifications. This should not to be taken lightly.

The moment you decide to start talking about your project is when you should also seek out the legal and tax advice of qualified professionals. After meeting with these professionals, you might find that operating your production company under the protection of a corporate entity, such as a corporation or the ever-popular Limited Liability Company (LLC), may provide liability safeguards of which you otherwise might not have been thinking about in your strategy.

The steps for setting up a business entity are pretty simple, but they could be costly depending on where you live. So again, as a general disclaimer, I am not qualified to offer legal or tax advice. So I can only talk about my own experience—which may or may not be right for you.

Establish Your Movie Website

Given the ways in which independent movie distribution is changing, having a great website for both your mini-studio and your movie is one of the most important aspects of your eventual movie marketing campaign. If you are not technical, the following guide should help.

The first step in your Internet movie marketing campaign involves reserving a domain name and hosting. To reserve space for your movie website, stop reading this book and head over to my friends at MovieSiteHost.com and reserve your hosting and domain name. And as a friendly disclosure, BlueHost pays me to promote their services. But I wouldn't recommend them unless I used them myself. For the past three years, I have utilized BlueHost hosting on all of my websites. And in the few instances when I needed to reach someone, the customer service was great and my calls were always answered.

Reserve Your Domain

Your domain name is often referred to as your website address. And for your movie website, your domain name should have the name of your movie in it. While I will share some tips on how to market and sell individual movie titles later in this book—in the event you want to reserve the domain names for your movies now—I recommend creating a domain name that reflects the title of your movie with the word "movie" after it.

For example, if you created a movie called about a career courier I recommend reserving CareerCourierTheMovie.com

Having your movie title included in your domain name helps people find your website. This is necessary, especially if your movie garners buzz. In those situations, it is very common for people to simply type in the name of your movie and see what shows up. Having your movie title included as part of your domain can help your movie show up in search results whenever anybody is searching for your movie.

Sometimes you will find out that your domain name is already taken. Assuming the name is not trademarked, you will have to decide if you want to change your movie title or modify the domain name. But if you cannot get a .com, I would strongly suggest avoiding other extensions like .net or .org. Unless you are part of a large nonprofit, those extensions are silly when it comes to movie marketing.

Website Platform

People throw around a bunch of silly jargon like Web 1.0 or Web 2.0 to describe the Internet evolution. But for the sake of your Internet movie marketing mastery, just know that websites are usually described as dynamic or static. A static website was all the rage in 1999. There was a time when your kid sister made crappy-looking HTML sites to serve as an online brochure, complete with crappy content.

Over the years, static websites have been slowly replaced by dynamic sites that can be updated frequently. One example of a dynamic site is a blog. As you probably know, a blog allows you to update your website with the ease of sending an email. At first blogs were mostly web-based diaries where people could share personal crap that nobody cared about. And then later blogs evolved to allow people to hone in on their niche and provide enormous value to like-minded enthusiasts.

To add to all this nerdy confusion, the delineation between blogs and standard, static HTML websites has gotten a little muddy. On top of this, most web nerds currently avoid using the words blog or website to describe their real estate on the net. Instead they now use the popular term, Content Management System or CMS, to describe websites. This sounds impressive and expensive, but a CMS is essentially blog technology that has evolved to the point where anybody can easily have an awesome website, fast.

The most popular CMS is WordPress. Many people choose to utilize the WordPress CMS because it is free, it is easy to use, and it is easy to customize. And because of these factors, many filmmakers can modify their sites to include sales pages, movie trailers, opt-in forms and other cool stuff. When you set up your site, I suggest forgoing old school static HTML sites and just set up all of your sites on the WordPress CMS platform.

Your Company Website

As mentioned previously, my affiliate for BlueHost found at MovieSiteHost.com allows you to reserve a domain name and hosting at the same time. After you reserve your domain name, your next step is to log into your account and click on an icon called "WordPress." From there, you will install WordPress on your server. After the three-minute installation, you will be issued with a username and a password. From there, you can log into the back office of your new website and begin your customization. Easy, right?

If what I just said confuses the heck out of you, then you have two choices. You can go through a learning curve or you can hire someone to do the WordPress installation and website customization for you. I know some friends who outsource these tasks through sites like fiverr.com or you can hire my firm at MarketYourMovie.com to help you get your site up and running. In my humble and very biased opinion, it may be beneficial to figure out how to set up your own hosting and domain. This way, when you start building individual websites for each of your movies, having familiarity with this type of stuff will help you save time and money. And in case you're wondering, MovieSiteHost.com will allow you to add-on additional domains under the same hosting account. This can save you a lot of money!

After you reserve your domain name and create an initial website, you will want to add some content to your site. This first version of your mini-movie studio website does not have to be complex, but should include the name of your company, your contact information for any press and traditional distributors. Then later, as you go into production on various movies, you will want to create a link from your company website to your individual movie websites, which we will cover later.

Movie Ideas

As a filmmaker, one of the reasons you make movies is to share your vision with the world. My suggestion is to determine if you would like to make money making movies. If so, do not make a movie unless you know your movie niche audience. If you do not care about making money with your movies, then you can simply say that you are doing it "for the love."

A few years back, I got involved in a project "for the love" without considering who would actually buy the movie. Guess what? The movie died. The movie did not make money. And several of my friends are still paying off their credit cards. That was stupid. Avoid this. I can tell you from experience that making movies is a lot more fun when you can cash checks.

So how do you improve your chances for making money with your movie? While nothing in life and business is guaranteed, you can improve your chance of success by focusing on and then finding you niche target audience. This process begins by defining your unique selling proposition. In traditional business, your USP is the one aspect of your product that sets you apart from the competition. In the movie business your USP is usually referred to as your hook. What is your hook?

The reason I want you to think about your USP early on is because through the course of your filmmaking career you will undoubtedly need to create relationships with prospective investors who more than likely make their living selling conventional products. So if you know how to put your movie business within the context of producing a general product, you will speed up rapport and build trust faster. You will enter into conversations, knowing you can speak the language.

Answer these questions:

1. What is your movie about?
2. Is there an audience for your subject matter?

Many filmmakers believe their movie will appeal to just about everybody. While I encourage you to think big, very few filmmakers have the marketing budget to reach a global audience. Instead, I advise you to take a more cost-effective approach to finding your niche target audience.

If there are print magazines devoted to your subject matter, then those subscribers are part of your target audience. If you cannot find a print magazine targeted to your niche, then odds are good that your niche is too small or not profitable. In addition to exploring the magazine rack, you can also conduct internet keyword research. To do this, go online and utilize a free Google tool called the: *Google Keyword Traffic Estimator* and find out if anybody is actually searching for your topic.

1. Google: "Google Traffic Estimator External."
2. Once you find the site, search keywords related to your niche topics. Make sure you put your keywords in quotes, like this: "Boxing Movie."
3. Hit submit.
4. Once you get results, look for a box on the left-hand side that says "EXACT." Click that box,
5. The search data will be displayed.

This information will let you know how many people are searching for terms related to your movie on a monthly basis. If there is a market for your movie, then your next step is to test your concept. One of the easiest ways to test your concept is through a crowdfunding campaign, which I will cover later.

Build Your Team

Once you have an idea of the types of movies you want to make, you need to create relationships with at least five to 10 collaborators who complement your skill set. At the very least, you'll want to find a writer who understands budgets, a physical producer experienced in production management, a tech guru who understands cameras and modern production gadgets, an editor with Final Cut Pro, and a sales and marketing professional and Internet guru who can promote and sell your movies online. You will also need a lawyer who can provide you with the necessary legal advice, contracts and guidance on setting up your mini-movie studio business.

If you look at my movie credits, you'll see that I've been working with the same crew on almost every project. This is not by accident. Making movies is challenging. And bringing unknown people into the process causes everything to become even more complicated. But you have to start somewhere.

So for those of you planning to crank out some movies, I recommend you start small. Find a few collaborators and assign jobs based on interest. Then grab a camera and complete some micro projects such as music videos, short films and funny sketches for YouTube.

A few months back, my buddy bought an HDSLR camera. Over a few afternoons, he tested the camera and edited the footage into two music videos that are now gaining popularity on YouTube. Creating manageable micro projects allowed him to make short movies that employ minimal locations, few actors and a lot of exteriors, which means he did not have to worry as much about the costs and time associated with interior lighting. The project was a lot of fun too.

On my website Filmmaking Stuff, people often ask me how to establish a team. If you are not in Los Angeles or New York, I suggest finding out if your state or country has a film commission. Often the film commission will have a film directory. I suggest getting a copy and then telephoning various people in the directory and asking to meet for lunch. For some filmmakers, picking up the phone and cold calling is challenging. So if you call and someone hangs up, it is a good indication that the prospect would not be good for your business anyway.

It continues to be my experience that most filmmakers are nice people and will respond favorably to like-minded creative folks. Assuming you make a few filmmaking friends, your next step is to complete some small projects together and, later, design a feature that can be explained in one high-concept logline. I personally favor original, genre-specific movies with a bit of controversy, geared toward a clearly defined target audience. But above all, your movie idea should be totally fun and captivating. (Otherwise, why make the movie?)

Test Your Team

Before you jump into BIG filmmaking projects, I recommend working with creative collaborators on weekend films and other smaller Backyard Indies. This helps you uncover everybody's idiosyncrasies early on. From this experience, you can determine whom you want to work with again on bigger projects. Utilizing test projects to uncover the bad apples is essential to your long-term filmmaking success.

A long time ago, I worked on a short movie with a guy. Long story short, I found out the guy was sleazy with money. He had hired one of my friends to build our movie website. But he failed to pay as agreed. When confronted, he shared an outlandish story about Western Union sending the money to the incorrect address. This was completely stupid and untruthful. Because he was a "friend," I gave him the benefit of doubt and dropped the subject. Three years later, I found myself working with this guy again. And guess what? He stole thousands of dollars from the movie budget. When confronted, he left Los Angeles for Kentucky or some other place. He did email a few times, apologizing. He was an idiot. I should have known.

Sometimes you uncover facts early on that could save headaches later. You need to have a forward-thinking perspective. In small deals, when you have moments of friction, your collaborators will often say: "This is not a big deal." But I now disagree. Frustrations on small projects will be amplified on BIG projects and may become really BIG problems.

Make Short Movies First

Before you make a feature, you should create a whole bunch of short movies. This advice is nothing new for the up-and-coming filmmaker. But what is new are the many options for distribution. In the past, most short films lived and died at film festivals. But these days, the Internet has changed everything.

With sites like YouTube, filmmakers are now able to find a global audience at the push of a button. In no previous time in history has it been so easy and inexpensive for filmmakers to get noticed. If you've never made a short film, the process is simple and fun. For your first few movies, don't worry about lighting or special effects. The goal of these projects is simply to take action and start doing. These small projects will enable you to utilize limited resources for maximum production value.

When you plan your movie, focus on a story you can tell in three minutes or less. In my opinion, comedy works best. When I was course managing a film program, I noticed a lot of first-time filmmakers created stories that focused on suicide or some troubled girl shaving her head and reminiscing about spiders. I even know one guy who made his friend hump a statue while wearing a gimp mask. (Don't ask.)

If you think you have a story like that, which you just HAVE to tell, by all means do so. But if you can be funny and get Internet viewers to share your movie with other people, who will then share your movie with other people, you will have achieved semi-famous greatness. All you need to get started is a camera, some friends and the ability to edit your footage.

To begin, write out a list of funny story ideas. Once you have a list, pick one that interests you the most. When you have it, call up some friends. Enlist them as actors and get to work. If most of your friends are preoccupied with marriage, a family and pregnancy, that's cool. Just start making movies starring you and your dog. (People love dogs.)

After a couple of these types of films, you may find yourself getting bored. This is actually a good sign, because it shows you're growing. When this happens, begin to create more complex stories and then write a well-crafted screenplay. Assuming you've been doing shorts with your friends, you will know who works well and who doesn't. Invite the best of your actor friends to your next movie.

Theoretically, if you make one or two three-minute movies like this every weekend for six months, you will have equivalent experience of making a feature. This short movie marathon will provide you with a fundamental understanding of how to shoot scenes for minimal cost and still make them interesting. This experience will help you save time and money when you create your feature, while providing you with endurance, experience and the confidence to make movies with efficiency.

When you upload your work for the world to watch, audience feedback will reveal areas needing improvement. Even though you're working with non-professional equipment and talent, if you can learn to make great movies with a small camera, you can make them with a big camera. When the feature filmmaker is ready, the feature will reveal itself. Short movies provide training. If you haven't made a short, get started!

Keep Your Day Job

If you have already made a couple of short films and know your way around a movie set, consider making survival money outside the industry. I know this sounds counterintuitive, but bearing in mind most filmmakers take crappy jobs or work as

PAs, getting well paid may be a good thing. Based on what I've been telling you, developing an ability to sell yourself and your talents is probably the most important aspect of your career. So before you wait tables or continue your career track toward Key Production Assistant, consider a job selling some sort of expensive product in a growing industry.

If you work for a good company, working a sales day job can pay really well. If you are lucky, you will mostly likely work from home, get to make friends, eat lunches for free, learn sales skills, and also have time in between legitimate client visits for motion picture meetings. Just make sure you save your money. Throughout the years, I have worked for various start-up companies in a sales capacity and some did not work out. Still, the upside to working outside the movie industry is the potential to make six figures a year. You can then dump that money into growing your movie business.

But know this. A good income can be the biggest downside of working outside of the movie industry. Many of your friends who struggle in entry-level positions within the industry will question your seriousness when you drive your brand-new BMW around town. While there is nothing wrong with being successful, your goal should be to free up your life so that you can make a comfortable living and then transition into a filmmaking role with the least amount of struggle. Additionally, if you find yourself working in a crappy day job for more than three years — and you still haven't made a movie (and still want to) — grow some balls and QUIT!

Chapter Two

Create Your Story

"Don't go around saying the world owes you a living. The world owes you nothing. It was here first."

–Mark Twain

To survive the volatility of modern moviemaking, you will have to change your strategy. As a filmmaker, you will need both a short-term game and a long-term game. Short term, you will obviously want to finish your feature film. Long term, you will need to think of yourself as a mini-studio, continually focused on building your brand, making more movies and growing your audience.

While creating a mini-studio may seem beyond the scope and scale of what you think is possible, setting your sights high is much more proactive than ignoring the fact that Backyard Indies now compete for the same virtual shelf space as mainstream Hollywood movies. As a result, much of your success as a modern moviemaker will involve increasing the amount of people who know you and your work. Because the market is saturated with competition, you must establish brand identity.

Branding is the marketing equivalent of matching your belt with your shoes. Don't make your marketing complicated. Make sure your colors, logos, posters and fonts are consistent. But at the same time, you must be mindful to create an exciting and memorable identity that represents the types of movies you enjoy making.

Research Your Concept

As a modern moviemaker, your success depends on your ability to create movies that people will actually pay money to see. Unless you have a gazillion dollars allocated to your marketing budget, it will be impossible to conduct a massive advertising campaign. However, in the world of Internet marketing, there is a saying that applies to your movie business: "Everybody is nobody, and niches will make you riches."

The first step to planning your movie and finding your niche begins with brainstorming a few movie ideas. Write down a list of at least a dozen movie concepts that seem interesting to you. From there, pick the most appealing idea. Keep in mind that getting your movie made, seen and sold is not a fast process. So in addition to creating a marketable concept, you have to love your material. If you cannot have fun with your story, then why make the movie?

Once you focus on a concept, you will need to distill your movie into one concise sentence known as a logline. For example, let's say your movie is described as "Zombies attack people." Obviously this is a very succinct logline, but it lacks the necessary detail to make your movie memorable. So your next job is to incorporate some flavorful elements into your logline. Here is the same example with added detail: "Zombies attack a camp for the mentally challenged."

While socially questionable, the extra detail adds sizzle to the description. This will help you in two ways. With a unique description, your prospective audience will immediately understand how your movie differs from all the other movies. And from a marketing perspective, the words "zombies," "zombies attack," and "zombie movies" will help target your core audience. Later, these targeted keywords will help you jumpstart your Internet search engine optimization campaign.

Target Your Market

Once you have your concept, take a moment to write down a few dozen niche specific keywords and phrases related to your movie. When you complete your keyword list, go to your computer and look up the Google Keyword Traffic Estimator External. Aside from having a long name, this is a free service offered by Google. And it allows you to find out exactly how many people search for you keywords per month.

Knowing how many people search for your target keywords will help you determine if your niche audience is large enough to support your movie budget. To demonstrate, let's pretend that your lifelong dream is to make a movie about purple pinecones. But after conducting your research, you sadly realize that only 12 people in the entire world enjoy purple pinecones. This means that in the best-case scenario, your core niche audience can only support 12 sales. But in reality, you will be lucky to convert one-tenth of 1 percent of your market into paying customers. As a result, you have to decide if your passion for purple pinecones is more important than your desire for dollars.

Assuming you are confident that your movie niche population is large enough to support your movie budget, your next goal is to locate blogs, websites and publications targeting your target audience. To get started, Google the keywords related to your movie concept. For example, if you had a boxing movie, you might Google the word "boxing." In doing this, you get more than 49 million results. This is not surprising.

Interests such as boxing, horror movies and martial arts have significant prominence in our culture. But if your movie focuses on more obscure subjects, you may have to dig deeper. Thankfully, even if your core audience is esoteric and comprised of a small global population, the Internet provides a great tool for reaching them.

Assuming you find publications targeting your audience, your next step is to create a spreadsheet containing the contact details of at least 100 related niche blogs, websites and print publications. Out of this list, determine your top 10 target publications. Reach out to these publications and request their subscriber demographic statistics. This information will further reveal niche specific information. These stats will often provide details on age and gender. This information will help you determine the appropriate marketing collateral.

Pick Your Story

It is beyond the scope of this book to explain how to become a great screenwriter. But because you are a modern moviemaker, I wanted to share a few thoughts about the importance of a acquiring and producing good script.

Your screenplay, above anything else mentioned in this book, is the most important element of your movie. Early in my career, somebody told me that the screenplay is the blueprint of the movie. And I totally agree. As a talented filmmaker, you have probably noticed that a lot of movies these days are crap. And if you have half a brain, you probably also think that you can do better. So to share some good news, you are correct!

A few years back, I read screenplays for a producer in New York City. During that time, I learned a few important lessons about all the screenplays floating around out there.

Lesson number one: Most screenplays on the market are crap. And I'm not just talking about scripts by new writers. I remember reading screenplays from working, established writers that seemed to be filled with underdeveloped characters, plots that didn't make sense and story ideas that were laughable. Add the enormous amount of material that came from friends of friends and other producers and it literally felt like my life was filled with screenplay garbage – because it was!

If you have any talent as a writer, the odds are stacked in your favor. Write a good script! And if you're not a writer, then find a good writer and team up with him or her. To do this, you may have to travel to your local film festival and seek out someone with talent who shares a similar moviemaking objective. If face-to-face networking is not a fit for your situation, you will have to leverage the Internet. Try Craigslist in the Los Angeles and New York City markets. Assuming you find someone who shares your vision, you will also want to create an agreement and then get the terms of your agreement on paper. The Writers Guild website offers sample agreements.

Remember, getting a movie made starts with the strength of your material. Weak material will give you weak results. Conversely, strong material can provide you with the leverage to approach "name" actors, prospective investors, agents, lawyers, other producers and fellow filmmaking collaborators. Having good material can help your project gain momentum.

Screenwriting

As a filmmaker, I assume you want to produce a movie and not just write or acquire a screenplay so you can sell it. So I am not going to focus on how to "sell" your screenplay. However, whether you plan on producing or selling your script, there are still a few factors applicable to either end-goal. The first thing you have to do is actually own the rights to a completed, polished screenplay. At the same time, you must understand that every element in your screenplay costs money.

So in addition to producing a wonderful story that speaks to your niche targeted audience, I recommend limiting your locations as well as the need for extensive use of your cast and crew. Additionally, it is essential to keep in mind that story elements such as ice, snow, rain, sunshine, dogs, lightning and children are challenging to predict. If you include any of these elements in your story, I can guarantee that setups that should only take minutes will take days. Limit their use if possible.

The other pitfall is trying to do too much with a limited budget. Many filmmakers attempt very expensive stunts, setups and special effects but lack the resources to execute properly. This oftentimes results in cheesy scenes (and sometimes, a cheesy movie). Stay within your budget. But at the same time, find creative ways to utilize the available props and locations to increase production value. Remember, your true genius will come from your ability to tell a compelling story, not by the expensive stuff you try to pack into your movie.

Once you have a solid draft, you will want to get some actors together and hold a table read. Hearing your screenplay acted aloud for the first time is an amazing experience. But as you begin showing off your script, just make sure anything you display to other people represents your best work. Remember, you only get one chance to make a good first impression. And that same thinking applies to your screenplay. You only get one opportunity to grab the attention of a prospective actor or investor who may decide to help you with your project.

Keep in mind that it's a Hollywood cliché that everybody has a screenplay. But this is simply not true. In my experience, most people in Hollywood only have the initial idea for a screenplay. Past that, maybe some of these "writers" have the first 10 pages for a screenplay. But that is it. So if you forget everything else from this book, please make sure you don't become another potential filmmaker with big ideas, but no material.

Sometimes the flipside is also true. I know a few filmmakers who got so excited about a project that they actually forget to read and refine the script to make sure it was actually good. I know this sounds silly. But it is true. This typically happens when a movie is fully financed and the production monies are in the bank. The desire to get into production becomes too great to resist. Money blown on a bad script can have disastrous consequences. My advice is this - Do not start production until you are sure the script is ready!

Here are 5 tips on getting your screenplay up to par:

1. Read and re-read. Each time ask yourself: "What else can I cut without compromising the story?"
2. Have other people read the script. If they can't find anything wrong, then you need new trusted readers.
3. Have a table read. If something sounds like crap, fix it fast! Seriously. You can't fix a bad script in post.
4. After the read, ask if anyone has feedback, good or bad. Take what works, ignore the rest.
5. Make every word push the story forward.

Make a Movie Poster

Having a movie poster was once essential for certain aspects of independent film funding. But as new options for independent movie distribution emerge, the need for a physical poster is becoming secondary to the broader focus of building a consistent online movie marketing presence. Despite this evolution, creating a poster is still a great starting point for your overall brand strategy. Later, elements from your poster will be used in creating your movie website, your promotional postcards, your DVD box cover and VOD thumbnails.

To get started, take some time to research successful movies in the same genre. Figure out what you like about the poster and artwork. Then hire your best graphic artist friend to create something that works for your title. And while you do not yet have your cast, creating an initial design concept that incorporates your logo, fonts and art will allow you to refine your marketing strategy. When it comes to movie marketing, your poster must influence the buying decision of your audience.

Create a Movie Website

As mentioned in the last chapter, I am a big fan of setting up a WordPress website to promote both my movie company and my movies. Assuming you follow the website set-up steps outlined in chapter one, you know that WordPress offers many easily customizable templates. And while many of the professional WordPress templates will work well for your production company website, I find most of these templates are limited when it comes to promoting individual movies. As a result, I recommend the "Filmmaker Theme" template for WordPress.

The goal of the Filmmaker Theme is to provide you with a simple, clean, fast way to set up a movie website. Once the Filmmaker Theme is installed, you will have the ability to easily add your trailer and links to your various VOD sales outlets. Additionally, the Filmmaker Theme allows you to change your site's background and add custom colors so that you can easily maintain brand consistency between your site and your other marketing materials.

I believe the Filmmaker Theme will revolutionize the ways in which filmmakers get their movies seen and sold. This is one of those ideas I have worked on for a long time. In fact, I cannot begin to tell you how many software developers flaked out in the process. But after a little persistence, I was finally able to gain some traction. If you would like to check out the Filmmaker Theme and find out how it helps you promote your movies, visit: IndieMovieSite.com.

Because the Filmmaker Theme operates on the WordPress platform, you will have the option to easily add extra functionality to your site through the use of widgets and plug-ins. These tools allow you to make your powerful movie website even more robust. For example, if you choose to install one of the many Twitter plugins, your followers will be automatically alerted every time your website is updated. Through a Google Analytics plug-in, you will be able to monitor your visitor data.

Start Blogging

Even with the greatest-looking movie website in the world, if nobody visits, you will not have a business. As a result, your primary online objective is to attract targeted traffic to your website. And while there are many methods to achieve this goal, one of the most cost-effective ways to attract traffic is to utilize the blog component of your movie website to publish frequent, relevant content. For example, if your movie is about toxic pollution, you will want to write blog articles related to environmental protection and toxic pollution.

To find topics relevant to your target audience, I suggest you revisit the Google Keyword Traffic Estimator and conduct some more keyword research. Your goal is to choose at least 100 relevant keyword phrases and add them to a spreadsheet.

These phrases will later be used in blog article titles and topics. Because many of your visitors will also be interested in participating in your filmmaking process, I recommend including a few articles that allow your readers to learn more about you and your movie project.

Once you have your article topics, make it a goal to publish new content at least three times a week. Keep in mind that most search engines are programmed to read text, so written articles are very search-engine friendly. But from a human perspective, each of your visitors will have a slightly different preference for how they consume content. So to serve the needs of your audience, I suggest peppering your blog with other types of content. What types of content?

In addition to writing content, I suggest grabbing a video camera and creating videos where you provide your visitors with updates on your movie-making progress. You can then upload these videos to your YouTube channel, grab the YouTube code and embed it in your blog as a new update. While you are in the process, why not separate and export the audio from your video? You could then upload the audio to one of the popular podcasting sites. All of this combined, over time, allows you to build a robust Internet footprint.

As you get closer to production, your need for frequent updates will increase. However, your focus will be shifting toward the actual movie making process. When this happens, I suggest you hire an intern or an assistant to help you maintain your content creation. If this is not feasible for your budget, you may choose to outsource some of your blog topics to ghostwriters. Or you might shift from writing to simply creating brief video updates. In addition to improved search engine rankings, good content also entices your fans to share your content with their social networks, which potentially drives more traffic back to your site.

Assuming you choose to install and utilize the Filmmaker Theme for WordPress, keeping the lines of communication open with your visitors is a cinch. In addition to the built-in blogging component, the Filmmaker Theme also invites visitors to comment on your articles. This means you can monitor your audience's reactions and respond when necessary. By allowing for two-way communication, you will have another tool to help you strengthen relationships. Once again, grab your copy of the filmmaker theme by visiting: IndieMovieSite.com

Build Your Audience List

Last year I gave a talk at the UCLA film school. And one of the students asked me why I emphasize audience list building so much. My answer? Given the disruption in traditional distribution sales channels, building an audience list for your movie and your career might be one of the most important decisions you ever make. Regardless of how much the independent movie industry changes, one constant will always hold true: YOU will need to get people watch your movie and hopefully pay you for this privilege. Your Audience List is your business.

As a modern moviemaker, it is vitally important that you focus on building long-term relationships with the people who know you, like you, and pay to watch your movies. And while it is nice to believe that all of your website's visitors will become lifelong fans, many will forget about you within minutes of clicking away. This means that aside from actually generating traffic to your website it is vitally important that you find a way to connect with your visitors long after the initial visit.

One of the easiest ways to increase your fan base is by creating online profiles within the various social networks and then asking your visitors to "Like you." But because many social networking sites run the risk of going out of vogue, it is vitally important that you get your visitors into a mailing database that you control. As mentioned earlier in this book, I recommend using a third-party email marketing service such as MailChimp or AWeber. These email-marketing services provide you with inexpensive ways to manage and communicate with your subscribers through email.

With that said, getting your visitors to subscribe to your email list is easier said than done. Think about it. Even though your movie is the most important project in your universe, most of your prospective fans are super busy with other priorities. In order to convince them to provide you with their email address, you will have to give them something of value for free. This is known as an "opt-in incentive." And a very common give-a-way is a download of the movie poster or some songs from your movie soundtrack.

To see an example of how I utilize opt-in incentives, visit FreeFilmmakingBook.com. You will immediately notice how filmmakers who sign up for the Filmmaking Stuff newsletter will receive over $47 in free filmmaking how-to products. Once you sign up, you will receive an email message from me asking to approve your subscription. Once you click the approval link, you will be redirected to a "Thank You" page that allows you to download all sorts of premium filmmaking tools for free. While I am obviously utilizing list-building to create a more meaningful relationship with you, this model should be applied to your own movie business.

Over the past few years, I have tested many email marketing companies. But out of all of them, I prefer a company called AWeber. (My affiliate link is AudienceList.com.) The reason I like AWeber is because they provide easy to use opt-in forms that you can quickly add to your website. They also have great customer service and, in my experience, emails sent from

AWeber have a high degree of deliverability. This is important because you actually want your email to arrive in a person's email inbox and not his or her spam folder.

But probably the most important tool that AWeber offers is something called a sequential email auto-responder. An auto-responder is a list of email messages that go out in whatever sequences you determine, automatically. This means you could pre-write a dozen movie-related emails and set up a sequence, whereby your fans will receive one email per day, an email per week or once a month. This is especially important during your production phase. Having an auto responder set up allows you to automatically stay in contact with your subscribers. If someone responds to your messages, these responses to your emails go into your inbox, like any other message.

Here are three tips for building your Audience List:

1. From now on, as soon as you have a website, start building your audience list.
2. Put your website on your business card.
3. Collect names and email addresses at screenings, networking events and film festivals.

Even with the best strategy, building an audience list large enough to support a movie career requires long-term perspective. It does not happen overnight. But even with this knowledge, many filmmakers quit their list before they get started or fall prey to bad strategies, like buying email lists.

Buying an email list is amateur hour. And it is just bad business. Aside from being extremely expensive, most times you will find that names and contact information on an email list is mostly useless. Additionally the people on these lists are not targeted, they don't know anything about you or your movie, and they never gave you permission to email them-which pretty much sounds like to spam to me. While it will take some time, you are much better off focusing your emailing campaigns on people who know you and want to support your moviemaking efforts.

Social Media for Modern Moviemakers

Just a few years ago, if you made a movie and failed to garner a great distribution deal, your movie would die in quiet obscurity without anybody ever knowing you were a filmmaker. But these days, through the use of social media, you can upload a few shorts on YouTube, create and publish to a blog, and, if you are lucky, have the opportunity to see your name known around the globe. So if I can share some advice with you, if you're just entering this new era of modern moviemaking, you have the chance to brand both your movies and yourself.

With that said, I will be the first to tell you that the words "social media" annoy me. Half the filmmakers talking about social media do not have any clue what it means or how to utilize it to promote movies. So right here and right now, I want to change that. In the old days, movie marketing was based on traditional media or one-way conversation. Guess what? I have a movie. So I am going to SHOUT at you through television, magazines, newspapers and website advertising in the hopes you will hear me, take action and buy my movie.

But social media is different. Social media is the online equivalent of having a two-way conversation with your fans. And unlike sophisticated, multi-gazillion dollar traditional advertising campaigns, social media can be produced anywhere, by anyone. It's word of mouth that you can monitor on the Internet. As a filmmaker, social media provides you with a way to monitor and measure the word-of-mouth marketing.

A few weeks back, I went out to a filmmaking event in Los Angeles. Even with my movie producing experience and Internet reach, I often spend most of my personal time hanging out with close friends and acquaintances. So when complete strangers at the event started approaching me, quoting some of my filmmaking articles and asking about my current projects, I had no idea how to react. It was the first time in my life when I experienced this. People I had never met knew me.

Without giving much thought to it, my Filmmaking Stuff website, podcasts, books and guest articles have defined me as a Modern Moviemaker. Over the last three years, through sharing my thoughts and ideas with the world, I have become somewhat "known." While I will be the first to talk about brand consistency in the context of one-on-one networking, I failed to realize that my Internet persona has weight in the physical world. This experience was an important reminder that the audience we engage consists of real people with dreams and desires.

With social media, you can create content and freely publish without asking for permission. In turn, your audience can respond, telling you what they think. So let's put this into context. Pretend that you produce a movie and release your first trailer on YouTube. Then you send out an email blast, a tweet and update to your friends on Facebook. In a matter of minutes, you will receive feedback on your trailer. And from these responses, you can participate in the conversation.

When I first started using social media, I made the mistake of throwing out a bunch of "look at me" one-way tweets. Like a lot of people, I thought I could just blast my Twitter followers with my message, and they would knock down walls to buy my stuff. I was wrong. Twitter is not TV. The minute you disregard the conversation is the minute you alienate your fans. The thing to remember is that the people you connect with via social media are real. And cultivating genuine relationships with your audience cannot be forced. So unless you have very deep pockets, your grassroots social media campaign will be spread over many months of audience engagement.

To help you put social media and audience engagement into perspective, I suggest you think of this in terms of going to a summer BBQ. When you socialize, you want people to like you and enjoy what you have to say. But if you do more talking than listening, you become "that guy." And speaking from experience, you don't want to be that guy (or girl)!

Facebook

Assuming you already have a personal profile, you know that Facebook allows you to easily stay in touch with friends, have conversations with co-workers, and find pictures of your ex-girlfriend. But from a promotional perspective, Facebook is also a powerful tool for filmmakers. If you are part of the Filmmaking Stuff community on Facebook, you may have noticed how filmmakers are free to reach out and share ideas with other filmmakers from all over the world. Facebook also provides you with a big opportunity to source and connect with your target audience.

To set up a Facebook profile for your movie, go to facebook.com and scroll to the bottom of the page. From there, click the link that says, "Create a page." You'll then be redirected to a web page that asks you to pick your page type. Assuming you're promoting a movie, choose "entertainment" and then pick "movie." Facebook will then ask you for the name of your movie. Afterwards, you'll log into your account. If you do not have an account (and you should), you'll have to create one.

Once complete, your movie page will be set. All you have to do is fill in pertinent information about your movie, including a description, photos, links to your movie website and, possibly, your movie trailer. Your next step is to reach out to your Facebook friends and invite them to "like" your movie. Depending on your genre and story, not all of your friends will respond to your request. Don't take it personally. Many of my movie projects have been ignored by friends. I tell myself it is probably because they are being inundated with various requests from Angry Birds, farmers and Mafia hitmen.

Assuming you can break through the noise, the advantage to utilizing Facebook to promote your movie is your ability to connect with your audience. Unlike BIG Hollywood powerplayers, your fans have access to you. This allows you to make their experience more personalized. By cultivating these relationships, your audience is more likely to promote your movie to their friends, which helps you build your fanbase and make more sales without spending much money.

In the event you would like to promote your movie further, Facebook provides you with targeted advertising opportunities to reach your target audience. For example, if you are promoting a zombie movie, you will actually have the ability to reach out to zombie enthusiasts and get them to "Like" your movie. Because they have demonstrated interest in the genre, your ability to build a relationship with these fans, and possibly get a sale, may increase.

One of the coolest aspects of building a Facebook fan page to promote your movie is the ease with which you can build buzz and create community around your title. Fans will be able to post content on the movie's page wall, and, as a result, you will be able to monitor what people are saying about your movie. And in the event you get spam, you can moderate comments.

In addition, some filmmakers allow fans to post photos to the fan pages. This sort of activity reinforces community and encourages word of mouth. For example, if your movie is on the festival circuit, you might ask your fans to post pictures from the screening. Then once the photo is posted, friends of these fans may see the picture—which may cause them to "like" your movie too. This way, the added social proof of like-minded fans touting the joys of your movie may increase your sales. This goes for Twitter and other online communities too.

Tweet This

Twitter is a social media site that allows filmmakers with an easy way to communicate and connect with fans. But the site is unique in the sense that it only allows you to send messages limited to 140 characters. These updates are called tweets. A Twitter account will allow you to answer questions from your fans and keep them up to date with your latest movie projects.

In my own movie business, I share blog posts, relevant articles, movie updates and ideas. I also utilize Twitter to connect with other prospective collaborators. The key to making Twitter work is dependent upon making sure that your tweets are interesting and engaging. You will also want to pay attention to what other people are saying and join the conversation. When successful, you will attract fans that care about you and your projects. Assuming you have interesting tweets, your fans will re-tweet your message to their followers. This allows you to spread ideas exponentially.

With that said, keep in mind that people do not want to be sold. People follow you because they are looking for interesting content, not another promotion. So assuming you are successful in building your Twitter following, you will want to be very subtle with your promotions.

When handled with care, you can utilize Twitter to gain audience participation in future movie releases and movie screenings. And as I will share later in this book, Twitter will also be an essential component to your future crowdfunding campaigns. Assuming you stay focused on keeping your followers happy, Twitter can provide you with an awesome return on your advertising investment.

Create a YouTube Channel

I often receive emails from filmmakers asking how they can get their work produced and seen. My response is always the same. Grab a camera, record something, and post to YouTube.

The reasons I emphasize YouTube is because the site is global. YouTube is owned by Google, which makes it a huge search engine, and the site has a social networking component built in. After you upload your video, other YouTube users can view your work, share it with their networks, and create community around your title.

Here are three steps to help you set up your YouTube Channel:

1. Go to YouTube.
2. Click "Create Account."
3. Once signed in, Click: "Upload."

In addition to YouTube, there are many other video sharing sites available. But for the sake of your movie business and this book, I am going to focus on YouTube. Setting up a YouTube channel is like having your own television station. Once set up, your goal is to upload videos that allow people to know you and your work. The ongoing objective with all of your social marketing is to build personal relationships with your audience. Even though you are well on your way to becoming a famous filmmaker, the key is to be authentic and personable.

As you move toward production, you may choose to videotape the process and share the videos on YouTube. This will allow you to include your viewers in the filmmaking process. Once engaged, many of these viewers may share your videos with their friends and social networks, which increases your Internet footprint globally. Many of these viewers may ultimately show their support by buying your movie.

Get LinkedIn

Over the past year, I really started using LinkedIn more and more to promote both myself and my projects. While LinkedIn has some of the same features as other social networking sites, the LinkedIn culture is geared toward business networking. This makes it vastly different than Twitter or Facebook.

As a result, the social rules are different. While it would make sense to post something funny, silly or stupid on Facebook, posting a similar message on LinkedIn may not be appropriate. Conversely, it would be strange to utilize Facebook in an attempt to get lunch meetings with prospective Hollywood Heavyweights whom you never met. But in the world of LinkedIn, as long as you're not a jerk, it is appropriate to seek and connect with prospects.

To get started, sign up for a profile at LinkedIn.com and reach out to people who know you and know your work. Once you establish this foundation, write out a list of at least 10 to 15 film industry professionals who may be able to help you with your movie business. Then do a LinkedIn search to find prospects.

Depending on the strength of your network, you may find that one of your contacts already has a relationship with your prospect. Your next step would be to reach out to your friend and ask if he or she would make an introduction. Assuming the introduction is made on your behalf, your prospect will be more receptive to hearing from you directly. Step-by-step, you can utilize LinkedIn to help you build your filmmaking team.

Movie Work Is Reality

While it is great to establish your social networking framework and create all the marketing material in the world, this is not enough get your movie made. My friend, the famed horror novelist (and screenwriter) Craig Spector once shared some advice with me that I have been rolling around in my mind ever since. I had just moved to New York City, and I was sleeping on my aunt's sofa. I had no idea what I was doing...

At the time, Craig was one of the few people I knew who was actually making a living with his creative work. One day I asked him what I needed to do in order to become successful. Never one to sugarcoat advice, he said:

"Work more. Do more. The work is reality. Nothing trumps reality."

Speaking from my experience in Los Angeles, I have met countless people who have great movie ideas. Some of them have dozens of Twitter followers and a movie website, but these people are not making movies. Why? Because these would-be filmmakers are searching for someone else to do the actual movie work for them. And the paradox is this: People won't help you unless you do the work. When it comes down to it, very few people are willing to put in the necessary sweat equity to actually finish a project.

Next thing you know, another decade passes, and you wake up realizing you haven't done any movie work. You have nothing but tweet. Tweet. Tweet.

Get off your ass. As I'll share in the next chapter, it is better to make something.

Chapter Three

Get Movie Money

"Innovation has nothing to do with how many R & D dollars you have. When Apple came up with the Mac, IBM was spending at least 100 times more on R & D. It's not about money. It's about the people you have, how you're led, and how much you get it."

–Steve Jobs

There is a time in every filmmaker's journey when making a feature film becomes a driving, burning desire! And making a feature is essential to your business success. Making your first feature is the rite of passage into the world of professional filmmaking. If done well, your first feature will be a significant step in an exciting career.

If you have written or control the rights to a fantastic movie script, you will need to figure out how much your movie is going to cost. Once the script is locked, any modification you make to the story or schedule—no matter how minor or major—will subsequently impact the budget. My veteran producer friend Forrest Murray taught me that the script, the schedule and budget are the same document. You'll need all three to make a movie. And in the process, if you change one document, you're actually changing all three. I'll chat about this some more later. For now, focus on your initial schedule so you can get to your budget.

Many motion picture professionals make a living just breaking down, scheduling and budgeting movies. So it's a pretty complicated and creative area. I recommend that you partner with a seasoned first assistant director or line producer who can guide you through the process. If this is not possible, you will have to learn how to break down and schedule your movie yourself. For this, I recommend researching Peter Marshall's Script Breakdown and Film Scheduling course. My affiliate link for this is: MovieScriptBreakDown.com

Breaking down the script means you will go through your screenplay, number each scene, and highlight each element, including locations, characters, props, make up, wardrobe, picture vehicles and special FX. After you highlight each element, you'll want to figure out when you want to commence production, as well as how long you plan to shoot.

You can determine this by choosing how many pages of your screenplay you plan to shoot per day. Then you can decide if you want to shoot five days on and two days off, or six days on and one day off. Or perhaps you will choose to shoot over a period of weekends. This is up to you. But regardless of what you choose, you need to make sure you plan everything. Again, all elements in the script, no matter how minor, will eventually impact your budget and your schedule.

Since many filmmakers would rather focus on the story than logistics, as soon as you decide to produce and possibly direct your movie, I suggest that you hire a seasoned Production Manager to work with you. These professionals are invaluable. They will read your script. And without fail, they will tell you that your movie is going to cost way more than you think! From there, they will help you alter the story to meet your budget constraints. Managing the budget is their job. Respect it.

Then ask your PM if they know a great first assistant director. The 1st AD will build off the Production Manager's budget and will schedule the movie. It is then the job of the 1st AD to keep the production on time.

In the event you lack both the money and the connections to hire someone to break down your screenplay and manage your movie, I recommend utilizing some of the great software tools available. The popular screenwriting program Final Draft offers an add-on called Tagger. Tagger allows you to go through the script and pick out elements and highlight them in various colors. Once all elements are selected, you can import this list into a scheduling software program.

Scheduling and Budgeting Software

There is plenty of filmmaking software to help you break down, schedule and budget your movie. The industry standard software is produced by Entertainment Partners, and it's called Movie Magic. The only downside to Movie Magic is the cost. To get both the scheduling and budgeting programs, you will shell out more than $500.

A few years back, I was one of the beta testers for a scheduling and budgeting program from Jungle Software called Gorilla. If you are creating an indie feature on a budget, this software will usually do the trick. Gorilla usually includes both a scheduling program and a budgeting program for a lot less money than some of the other software tools.

As an alternative to desktop-based software programs, there are quite a few Internet-based tools gaining popularity. One of the latest programs to enter the scene is called LightSPEED eps. In addition to being an awesome script breakdown and scheduling program, LightSPEED eps allows you to centralize your production information and provide secure access from your computer, wireless device, from anywhere in the world.

Like a lot of companies mentioned in this book, it should come as no surprise that I have created an affiliate relationship with LightSPEED eps. Should you wish to try out the system for one of your projects, I will receive compensation. On the same token, the company has made their service affordable for independent filmmakers. Go to: IndieProductionTool.com

Regardless of your tools or methods, the reason you will need an initial schedule is because this information will help you determine your budget.

Define the Scale

Once you complete your initial breakdown schedule, you will then plug the information into your budget. As each element has an associated cost, it will become apparent which elements require the most cash. In this sense, you will have a birds-eye view of your movie in terms of scope and scale. Assuming you planned for an ideal execution of your movie, your project will cost considerably more money than you probably actually have. When this happens, you have a few choices.

1. Plan on getting a lot more money.
2. Rewrite the screenplay for a cheaper budget.
3. Modify or cut the budget!

But before you alter your story or your budget, I recommend reaching out to your network and asking for help. Let everyone know you are making a movie. And then provide a list of everything you need. Most filmmakers can find deals on food, locations, special FX, picture vehicles and other props. Chances are that someone you know knows someone who has what you need. And depending on where you shoot, you may be able to get these elements for FREE or at least get a discounted rate.

Even if you do not have money, think creatively.

Do you have friends who own locations you can utilize for free? Do you have access to discounted equipment? Can you finish your movie ahead of schedule? Do you have a friend with an edit suite? Can you shoot some scenes outside during the day to reduce the need for extra lights? Can you find free food for your cast and crew? Does one of your partners own a camera and lighting company? These are just some of the ways you can reduce your expenses.

One of my buddies was able to do this on the cheap. He had a location budgeted for $5K. However, after my buddy spoke with the owner of the location, the fee was reduced to zero. How? My buddy agreed to shoot a promo for the owner's business. Another filmmaker friend got free food for his entire shoot simply by asking. The food supplier was thanked in the credits. Deals happen. Creativity is essential for opportunity.

Once you have an idea of what elements you can get for free or at a significant discount, you can then add this information to your budget. If this is your first feature film, I suggest creating a budget for your movie in the arbitrary neighborhood of $300K. The reason I like this budget range is that is allows greater opportunity for return. In other words, a penny saved is a penny earned. And the more money you spend, the more money you have to recoup.

Get Legal Help

Before I go further, let me remind you of something important. As a disclaimer, I am not qualified to offer investment or legal or financial advice. Everything I tell you in this book is based on my personal experience. What works for me may not work for you or other people. Always talk with a qualified professional before embarking on any endeavor.

Whew...

I include the above disclaimer because in the movie business one lawsuit has turned many first-feature dreams into never-ending nightmares. So before you meet with prospective investors to discuss the magnificent merits of your movie project, talk with qualified legal and tax professionals to find out how to conduct your movie money-raising campaign ethically and legally. But at the same time, be careful. There are many types of lawyers in this world, and some of them are complete jerks.

A few years back I finished the first draft of my first screenplay. Like a lot of folks who dream of Hollywood success, I was eager to share my work with the world. Problem was that I had no idea what I was doing. Through a friend of a friend, I was put in contact with an "entertainment attorney." I put the words in quotes because, while there are tons of people with a strong work ethic and great integrity, this particular guy was not one of them.

I remember getting off the phone. I was super excited because this guy had agreed to read my screenplay and offer me feedback. So like most writers, I sent off my screenplay packaged with the appropriate cardstock cover and two brass brads.

A few weeks later I get the following email:

"Jason. Thanks for sending me your screenplay. I read it. Because you want to produce your own movie, I think you will need a lawyer who understands how to put together a private placement memorandum. And also, while we did not talk about this prior, you owe me $250 for the hour I spent reading your script. Please send me a check ASAP."

These days I would tell him to go "F" himself. But back then, I had no idea what I was doing. So I sent him his money. And to make it even worse, at the time I was very poor, and $250 represented an entire week's salary. The whole point of this is—before you get into business with ANYBODY—it is best to outline the job and also get reciprocal expectations in writing.

This rule is especially important when raising money. If you go the conventional route of putting together a common investor package called a private placement memorandum, you will want to delegate this to a lawyer with experience in the indie film industry and securities.

How Do I Get the Money?

One of the biggest reasons I felt compelled to write this book was so that I could share some simple tips on how to meet and build relationships with investors. When I first started, I used to ask everyone how to get money to make movies. Back then, most folks responded to me as if I were seeking the fountain of youth. The more I asked, the less people told me. I thought it was bizarre. It took my moving to New York and working with an indie producer to finally get the answers I was seeking.

Other books and filmmaking DVDs tell you that one popular way to raise movie money involves convincing dentists, doctors and lawyers to fork over cash. In this model, you are supposed to sell these people on the excitement of filmmaking and promise that, even though the movie won't make money, there will be a really cool wrap party and premiere. Let me get this straight…You plan to ask people to throw tens or even hundreds of thousands of dollars of their hard-earned money at a movie just so that they can attend some party?

In order for this strategy to work, your prospective investor has to be extremely wealthy, risky or a little crazy to participate. I am not saying these people don't exist and that these methods don't work—they totally do. Hollywood is filled with stories of multi-zillionaires who trade their money for the opportunity to experience fame and fortune. And while I do not know any of these reckless investors personally, I am pretty sure these types of people can be found every day in Vegas at the high rollers Blackjack table. But these folks are in the minority.

Most prospective investors are seasoned business professionals who manage their money in a superb way. They have run successful enterprises and will try to evaluate your movie business through this paradigm. As mentioned many times in this book, your movie is your business! And like any business, if you present a project with inexperienced management, lack of star talent, no distribution strategy in place, and no clue on how you'll get a return the money, prospective investors will quickly realize the inherent risks of your project. This is assuming you can finish the movie on time and on budget.

While risk tolerance is different for every investor, your project becomes more appealing if you find ways to convey an upside (including the possibility for fame and fortune) for minimal risk. In this regard, one of your biggest challenges is to make your movie good business. If you're pitching a business project that has no revenue-generating framework—meaning that your movie is not yet made and there is no plan for eventual distribution—you will need to refine your selling points way past the possibility of throwing a wrap-up party to make your project appealing.

For perspective, suppose you were going to open an ice-cream shop. In this scenario, a prospective investor could compare your ice-cream business plan to another, similar ice-cream shop catering to a similar population in a similar town somewhere else in the world. These numbers would provide investors with an idea of how your ice-cream business may perform.

Develop Your Personal Brand

Before you start telephoning prospective investors with your movie idea, you need to first grasp the concept of personal branding. And while I don't expect you to start selling t-shirts with your face, becoming conscious of how you are perceived is essential to your success with prospective investors and heavy hitters. And this is important.

Over the years, I have noticed that many people do not pay attention to how other people perceive them. Most people who want a career making movies fail because they never give thought to how they want to be perceived professionally. These people are the ones who talk a big game, but most often never deliver. They associate with the wrong people. They lose focus and direction. And they tarnish their reputations by having no consistency of character.

For example, when I had my first job in New York City as a production assistant, I was working alongside another PA who kept telling me she was a producer in North Carolina. All day, as we fetched coffee and lemon-lime seltzer water, she kept telling me how hard she was working. She also attempted to boss me around, asking me to do her work while she called her friends on her cell phone. Eventually, someone caught on that this "hard-working producer" wasn't doing too much work, and she got the boot. This is a poorly managed brand.

If someone thinks he or she is a serious, hard worker, but everyone else thinks this person is lazy and unprofessional, then something is way off. To avoid this type of disconnect, it is paramount that you create an identity consistent with the person you want to become. Then, work your butt off to make sure you become that person. Powerful people act in ways consistent with how they want to be perceived. Now, I want you to compare the person you are now to the person you want to become. Take a moment to project into the future and visualize the ideal life for yourself. What is a good plan for your movie business? How do you see yourself in five years?

Figure out small steps you can take today to ensure that your thoughts and actions are congruent with the future you. For example, if you want to become a hard-working, efficient power player, going out until 4 a.m. and then sleeping all day is probably not the best way to achieve your goal. As you start to become conscious of this type of stuff, you can eliminate current habits that will prevent you from becoming your idealized future you. Try to take small steps every day and, after a couple months of doing this, you will get closer and closer to becoming the person you want to become. Your life will be filled with dream opportunities.

Your Circle of Influence

In addition to personal brand management and maintaining a philosophy of never asking permission to create your world, creating friendships with powerful people will accelerate your Hollywood success. It's not advertised, but most Hollywood people are accessible. However, their time is valuable. So before you make any contact, you need to first focus on the WIIFM (What's In It For Me?) proposition.

If you preemptively seek out ways to answer the WIIFM proposition and focus on adding value to the other people's lives (while expecting nothing in return), making powerful friends is easy. From now on, whenever you meet someone new, just remember to take genuine interest in what this person has to say. Listen more than talk. Find out this person's wants. Perhaps you can put this person in contact with someone who can help to make this happen.

The flip side of this is also true. Birds of a feather do flock together. So if you get into a situation where you're just not connecting with people, leave. Seriously. There is no greater waste of your precious time than spending it with people who do not complement your vision. This is important in your personal life. This is especially true in the filmmaking business.

Manage Your Reputation

Making friends and forming alliances with other folks in the motion picture industry is essential for your success. From the first time you set foot on a movie set as a production assistant to the time when you start production on your fifth feature, you will need to enlist the help of other people. If you fail to cultivate a good reputation for yourself, success will become considerably more difficult.

Your reputation and how you present and sell yourself, your talents and your skills is everything. If people do not like you, it will be very difficult to realize your filmmaking dreams.

So starting today, you need to assess yourself. Do people typically like you? Do people go out of their way to help you? If not, then you now know one area you can improve is in your dealings with others.

But even if you are already considered likable, there is always room for improvement. So my suggestion is to start working today to become more well-rounded, friendly and helpful in everything you do. Over time, being known as a hardworking, likable person will help you navigate Hollywood.

Network without Becoming a Jerk

Picture this. You're at a film festival party. Someone approaches you, gets your name, and then asks the same question that always comes up: "What you do?" As soon as you tell the other person, there is a beat, the moment or two when the person decides if you are worth his or her time. If not, then the other person will feign a polite interest in you, look over your shoulder for someone more important to talk to, and leave the scene, tossing you a business card on his way out. Sound familiar?

In the past, whenever someone mentioned the word "networking" to me, the mental picture that always came into focus often involved some idiotic, overly energetic schmoozer who hands out business cards like candy. These people typically have their own agenda and could care less about you—unless they could use you. While this strategy may be utilized by many up-and-coming filmmakers and obnoxious amateurs, I promise you that this will not be your method. Personally, I think these users are annoying, full of hot air, and suck my social energy. I recommend that filmmakers never employ this type of silliness. To avoid becoming a walking business card dispensary, I want you to focus on one question every time you think about networking: How can you HELP the other person?

If you like the other person and think they are a nice human being, I want you to always focus on finding ways to help. By helping other people reach their goals, all the lessons we spoke about (rapport, reputation and building relationships) will work in your favor. Help enough people, and enough people will help you. Simple, right?

Build Unforgettable Rapport

You'll hear this a lot from me, but if you cannot connect with people and build relationships, garnering any measure of success in the movie industry will be difficult. In other words, for people to do business with you, it really, really helps if they like you. But let's be honest, sometimes it's just downright difficult to connect with some people. It takes energy. Sometimes conversation is a lot like pulling teeth. So in these situations, what do you do?

Well the good news is you can apply a few minor tweaks, strategies, techniques and communicative psychology to your social style. And this stuff can open the door to many meaningful and profitable relationships with Hollywood folks and investors, giving you an edge over people who don't know this. Rapport is simply a feeling of connection between you and the person (or people) around you. Establishing rapport is the first step in creating a Hollywood relationship. Thankfully, it's easy.

The first thing you need to do is read the trade journals and national newspapers and watch the news whenever you can. This will keep you informed of current events, including sports, finance and especially entertainment. Why? Because when you're informed, finding conversational topics with strangers will come easier—a skill you'll need if you ever meet prospective investors or Hollywood heavyweights.

In Hollywood, there are two trade journals: Variety and The Hollywood Reporter. Read them! Additionally, you should read business and success books unrelated to filmmaking. I recommend: How to Win Friends and Influence People and Never Eat Alone. Also, since communication is mostly body language, one effective technique to building rapport involves mirroring and moving your body in sync with the person with whom you're talking. Just a word of caution: Don't be obvious.

As you meet more people, you will begin to expand your context of what is possible in life. People will provide you with ideas and often introduce you to other people. Add this up over time and you'll soon see how each person you meet potentially creates a positive ripple effect that will propel you in the direction of your Hollywood Movie Making goals!

I am sure you heard that it isn't what you know that counts, but who you know. And if you don't know the right people, earning money making movies will be difficult! But how do you go out and meet friends, find investors, and influence Hollywood people? Wouldn't it be great to contact Hollywood heavyweights who have never heard of you and get a meeting? Or perhaps you want to meet the famous millionaire in your hometown where you grew up.

Would you simply pick up the phone and call those folks? What would you say? What's in it for them to meet with you? Sound overwhelming?

When I was starting out, I had all these questions too. In addition to making movies, I spent five years working as an account executive for one of the biggest investment banks in the world. During that time, I learned some cutting- edge strategies for getting meetings with important people. For example, did you know that, on average, it takes seven face-to-face meetings to establish a business relationship? Yep. Read that again. Seven meetings! If you follow these secrets, it's simple.

Meet Rich People

If you hold the general belief that rich people are in some way greedy and unwilling to help anyone, think again. Aside from a few rotten apples and idiots, the statistics show that wealthy people are quite generous, kind and hard working.

Why is having a positive attitude toward the affluent important for filmmakers? Unless your movies are financed and distributed by a studio, you will need to learn how to raise money for your own projects. You will also want to know what prospective investors look for in a project. When it comes time to shake the money tree, it would be helpful to have a few rich people just a phone call away.

Meeting and building relationships with rich and successful people is actually easier than you think. The first thing you need to do is ask around your home town and find out if anyone knows rich people. It seems to me that every town in the U.S. has at least one person a little better off than the rest. Once you find these people, your next step is to find out everything you can about them. Develop a plan for meeting them and asking some very solid questions.

After that, do some research, find a phone number, and then dial the digits. Most likely you will reach an assistant. So be prepared to leave a message. Explain that you are a first-time entrepreneur. Find out if they would meet you for a few minutes so you can ask for advice. Until you get your legal paperwork in order, your goal is to ask for advice, not money!

Assuming you get the meeting, show up in nice clothing. Shake hands with a firm handshake and keep your eye on the clock. Utilize some of your rapport building skills. If successful, the meeting will turn to you. Explain how you have a goal of producing a movie in your home town. And then ask this question: "If you had a goal of making a movie, what do you think prospective investors would want to know in order to back the project?" Then shut your mouth and take notes!

Many of these busy folks will reject the meeting. If this happens, move on. Find someone else in your network. Then as the months go by, cultivate a friendship. Remember, it takes an average of seven attempts with a prospect to get a meeting. Most filmmakers give up after the first rejection. As long as you apply a little persistence, you'll be surprised whom you can meet and what you'll accomplish. As your relationships with successful people mature, they may someday introduce you to their friends, who may become interested in your next project.

Hollywood Money 101

One of the lessons I have learned through the years is that my successful filmmaking friends do not work for money. They make money work for them. If you adopt a similar philosophy, over time you can free up your life and focus on filmmaking. This may seem easier said than done. But the main reason most investors become investors is because they have superior financial intelligence. And the reason most people go broke is because they have superior financial ignorance. The goal is to become smarter about money. With time and with luck, perhaps one day you'll be able to bankroll your own movies!

If you want to raise money for your movies, chances are you will have a few meetings with prospective investors. And when you get into a conversation, you may quickly realize that many of these folks have a tendency to speak the language of business. Peppered throughout this language are common financial terms. You need to know these terms so you can speak their language. If you do not know what they are talking about, you could severely handicap your money-raising potential.

Below I have listed some of the most commonly used business terms to serve as a foundation for your financial education.

Asset: You own something that makes you money. This could be a business you aren't required to work at every day, a stock that pays a dividend, investment real estate that provides checks each month or profit points in a movie that actually makes money.

Liability: You own, rent or use something that provides someone else with income. Examples would be credit card debt, your car loan or your home loan. One of the cool aspects of accounting is the relationship between things. Your liability is usually somebody else's asset. For example, if you rent an apartment, your apartment is your liability, but it is also your landlord's asset.

Cash Flow: Cash flows in, and cash flows out. When it flows out, it's called negative cash flow. When it flows in, it's called positive cash flow. Assets provide positive cash flow in the form of income. And liabilities create negative cash flow in the form of expenses. With your movies, you can choose to keep the rights to your movie, sell DVDs, and collect you income each month.

Capital Gain: You owned an asset or a liability and were able to sell at a profit. For example, let's pretend you fixed up an apartment house and "flipped it." When you sell your property for more than you invested, you have created a capital gain. In a movie scenario, if you were fortunate enough to sell off all rights to your movie for a lump sum, you would create a capital gain.

Equity: Another word for equity is ownership. Let's say your investor comes into your project for a 1/4th ownership. In this scenario, your investor would own 25 percent of the equity.

Establish Income

In the film business there are several different categories of income. As you progress through the movie business, your income may come as Earned, Passive or Portfolio. The differences between these incomes are important, because the way you make money can affect the way Uncle Sam taxes you.

Earned Income

This is the most common way people make money in Hollywood. To make money this way, you simply trade your time for money. You get a job. You only get paid when you show up. If you get sick or break a leg and miss work, you will be out of luck. And when you compare this to the other income categories, Earned Income is taxed pretty hard.

If you're working as a freelancer in the United States, you rest assured you will get smacked with the additional self-employment tax. Some folks call this "the double whammy." Taxes aside, most of us were raised to believe time is money. But you're different. I assume you want to live the good life and make movies. Promise yourself you will stop trading your life for money. The way you do this is simple. Replace Earned Income with Hollywood's golden goose…

Passive Income

Passive Income is money that flows to you without you having to work for it, which in my opinion is one of the best ways to make money. Passive Income doesn't care if you sit around in your underwear and do absolutely nothing; once you have a steady stream of Passive Income, the hardest job you'll ever have is cashing checks. As a filmmaker, your movie can become a vehicle for Passive Income. Most filmmakers focus only on the big payout. However, depending on your distribution deal, an alternative to selling your rights for a lump sum is to create an income stream.

It may be too early for this type of strategy, but I want to get you thinking. In the event you create a project that could potentially provide enough Passive Income to pay your mortgage for the next few years, it may be worth considering. A subcategory of Passive Income in Hollywood is called...

Residual Income

Residual Income flows to you when you own movie rights, song rights, a patent, a book or when you had a nice acting gig in a SAG movie. Everybody loves residuals!

In this scenario, you get a paycheck every time these properties are screened, heard or otherwise utilized. Hollywood Heavyweights often forgo Earned Income for Residual Income when they work on a project and negotiate ownership points. In many cases, one point will be equal to one-percent of the budget. If the movie makes money, then anyone who owns points will get a percentage of the profits. These back-end deals add up. Established players with a track record can create financial freedom.

Portfolio Income

Portfolio Income is generated from owning stocks and bonds. Bonds can provide you with an income stream, and stocks can pay out earnings called dividends.

Over time, if you convert your Earned Income into stocks and bonds, you could end up with enough Passive Income to pay for your desired lifestyle. Of course, if you go into portfolio investments without consulting a qualified and skilled professional, you could lose everything.

But I don't want you to lose money! I want you to make it. So learn and live this new mantra: "Every Hollywood dollar I earn is my money assistant. I find creative ways to make my money make more money while I sleep."

Business Plan

Many feature filmmakers get overwhelmed when they start thinking about how they will make, market and sell their movie. To help you overcome this challenge, I recommend that you write a business plan for your movie. While there are many software programs that can help you structure the format of a formal filmmaking business plan, here are the basics:

1. Who is behind this project?
2. What's the market like?
3. Describe your motion picture company.
4. Who is involved in the management?
5. How will you market and sell your movie?
6. How much money will you need?
7. Where will you spend it?
8. How do you expect to return the money?

Even knowing these elements, most traditional filmmaking business plans are incomplete. Until five years ago, distribution was discriminatory. This meant that many filmmakers seeking funding were unable to create a marketing, sales and distribution plan that they could implement. So instead of creating a useful sales strategy, many Hollywood hopefuls settled for the Sundance lottery. This is a risky gamble.

Fortunately, as a result of the Internet evolution, you now have the ability to freely access the marketplace. By paying a one-time upfront fee, companies like Distribber allow you to access the most popular marketplaces. This provides you with a way to create a business plan and marketing strategy with a fully accessible sales channel. Having a marketing strategy makes conversations with prospective investors much easier. So as you start thinking about your modern movie business, I recommend you answer these questions:

1. Who is your Target Audience?
2. How large is your Target Audience?
3. How will you reach your Target Audience?
4. What is your marketing strategy?
5. How many VOD sales to break even?

The actual mechanics of writing a business plan are not too complicated. And thankfully there are many books, templates and software tools available to make the process easy. One of the business plan tools that I get paid to recommend can be downloaded at MoviePlanPro.com. With this tool, you will be provided with an easy-to-use business plan outline.

Crunch the Numbers

Truth be told, math is a weak subject for me — and I dare say, most of the filmmakers I know. However, there are many spreadsheet templates that allow you to budget and project the marketing return on investment for your movie. To give you an example of how this works, here is a formula that I use early in my process to ballpark my marketing expenses.

In the following marketing ROI formula, I simply plug in some estimated costs related to pay-per-visit advertising. With pay-per-visit advertising, you pay for targeted visits to your movie website. This type of advertising works well if you have a movie with a dose of controversy and a strong hook. But even if you have the best movie on earth, only a small percentage of your web visitors will buy. So for the following scenario, I am assuming that only 1 percent of the visitors will buy. The next question is: How many visits will you need to sell 100 units of your movie?

> 100 units = Our goal for this ad campaign
> $.05 = Amount you may pay advertiser per visit.
> (StumbleUpon advertising rate)
>
> X = Number of Visitors needed for 100 units if only 1 percent buy
>
> (X).01 = 100 units
> EQUATES TO: X= 10,000
> THEN 10,000($.05) = $500 paid for targeted traffic

So in other words, if you were lucky enough to get a one-percent conversion, you would have to pay $500 in pay-per-visit advertising to sell 100 units of your movie. But let's go one step further. Let's assume you hate order fulfillment and shipping. So you decide to let a company like Amazon's Create Space or iTunes, or other totally awesome, popular marketplace handle your order.

Video on Demand for Rent

> 100 units ($3) = $300 – 50 percent to marketplace = $150
> minus $500 paid for advertising = NEGATIVE $350

Ouch! In this VOD rental scenario, the pay-per-visit ad numbers don't work—unless you like losing money.

Video on Demand for Download

> 100 units ($10) = $1000 – 50 percent to marketplace = $500
> minus $500 paid for advertising = BREAK EVEN

Again, ouch. In this VOD download to own scenario, the numbers work a little bit better. Assuming you're lucky enough to get one-percent of your money returned, at least the advertising pays for itself. But unless you can sell your VOD download for more money, get a better advertising deal, pay less to the marketplace or increase conversions by a much greater percentage than one-percent, pay-per-visit advertising is going to be a difficult method for returning money to your investors.

Direct DVD Sales

While I'm messing around with numbers, let's do another projection. Even though the world of DVD is fading fast into our memory - Let's go ahead and use the same formula to find out what it would take to churn a profit with direct DVD sales.

> 100 units ($20) = $2000 – 50 percent to marketplace = $1K
> minus $500 paid for advertising = $500 in PROFIT

Ah ha! If you're fortunate enough to get 1 percent return on your pay-per-visit advertising, you can see how physical DVDs sold at $20 a pop may offer a slight profit margin. In other words, in this scenario, for every 50 cents spent, you get $1.

So let's tackle the bigger problem. Let's try to get a return on our $1 million movie selling physical DVDs, while using pay-per-visit advertising alone:

> Movie Budget = $1 Million
> Physical DVD Sales using Pay Per Visit Advertising
> $1,000,000 divided by $20 per unit = 50,000 Units

This number represents a lot of units!

Since we will pay close to 50 percent of all transactions for the privilege of doing business within the marketplace, we will actually have to sell twice as many units (100,000 units) to make up for marketplace costs, and hopefully make a profit.

> 100,000 units = Our goal for this ad campaign.
> (A huge number!)
>
> $.05 = Amount you may pay the advertiser per visit
> X = Number of Visitors Needed to buy 100,000 units if only 1 percent buy
>
> (X).01 = 100,000 units
> EQUATES: X= 10,000,000 (Yes, TEN MILLION people!)
> THEN 10,000,000($.05) = $500,000 paid for targeted traffic
>
> 100,000 units ($20) = $2,000,000 – 50 percent paid to marketplace = $1,000,000 minus $500,000 paid for advertising = $500,000 in profit.

So to break even, you would need to sell 100,000 units and bring in $2,000,000. WOW! This is going to be challenging. Seriously. Is this realistic?

Based on this scenario, as a filmmaker you will (obviously) need to expand your promotion beyond pay-per-visit advertising! I will share some other marketing tips later in this book. Because distribution has become non-discriminatory, YOU must treat your modern movie business like a serious business.

You will need to sit down with a calculator and find the marketing strategy that works best for your movie and crunch numbers until they work. Out of this research, you will then create a marketing component for your business plan. And after that, you will need to budget for these marketing costs.

While there are no guarantees in any business, having a plan for marketing, sales and distribution sure beats the old days when the most popular plan for ROI involved crossing your fingers, and praying that you would win the Sundance lottery.

Small Business Filmmaking

These days, treating your movie business like any small business simply means you do not need to ask for permission to access the marketplace. You can make your movie NOW! And your prospective investors might take notice.

Here are some ways you could eliminate the downside for prospective investors:

1. Control the rights to a great script.
2. Attach name actors to your project.
3. Have a traditional distribution deal in place.
4. Attach an experienced director and cinematographer.
5. Attach an experienced line producer and 1st AD.

Even though some filmmakers think getting money is somehow limited to the arena of filmmaking, it's not. The truth is all budding business professionals need to shake the money tree from time to time. So luckily for us filmmakers, the world of business provides us resources for getting money.

The traditional ways people raise money in the United States (aside from going to a bank) is by meeting with an attorney, putting together some complex paperwork in-line with the Securities and Exchange Commission regulations, meeting with potential investors and building a relationship, and then asking for money. Hopefully, this will be followed by a signed check! Now, this is pretty complex. So I hope you've taken some time to look at your movie. Do you need a few million to make your film? Or if you're really creative, can your project be made for much less? This will determine your strategy.

If you've worked really hard to eliminate costs in your budget, then it's possible to make a fancy-looking movie for less than the budget. In many situations, you can replace cash limitations with creativity. But keep in mind that there are laws, rules and regulations that regulate how you will run your business. This means you'll need to know a few things about protecting yourself and your business from liability. Fortunately, once you acquire skills and confidence in your ability to attract and retain an audience and make money, you will get very used to running your filmmaking as a business.

Crowdfunding

If you have read my website Filmmaking Stuff for any length of time, you will probably notice I talk a lot about "sourcing an audience." After having a discussion on the topic with one of my clients, it occurred to me that most filmmakers have no idea what I am talking about. So let me break it down.

In the old days, making, marketing and selling your movies required that you knew someone in Hollywood with a lot of money. It also meant that you waited around forever for some traditional distributor to validate your existence and hopefully pick up your movie with something other than a crappy deal.

But that was then. These days, you do not need to know anybody in Hollywood. You don't need a gazillion dollars. And thankfully you no longer need some traditional movie distributor to give you permission to make, market and sell your movie. While these changes make this an awesome time to make movies, the new challenge is finding people willing to pay money to watch your movie. So how do you a source an audience? I will give you one word: Crowdfunding.

What is crowdfunding? According to Wikipedia, "crowdfunding describes the collective cooperation, attention and trust by people who network and pool their money and other resources together, usually via the Internet, to support efforts initiated by other people or organizations." In short, this means filmmakers finally have a new way to raise money.

Filmmakers can set up profiles at various crowdfunding websites and then easily promote their movie project via their social networks and ask for money. In exchange for money, filmmakers offer tiered incentives to prospective sponsors. For example, in exchange for some donating 10 bucks to your project, you might offer a promotional t-shirt and a DVD. For 500 bucks, you might offer a flight to the premiere.

Crowdfunding in this context is NOT the same as seeking equity investors, which makes this a very uncomplicated way to find sponsors and raise money. But outside of this obvious use, there is a little known secret about crowdfunding.

Let's say you're a filmmaker with an idea for a movie. And let's suggest that you aren't sure how many people would be interested in your movie… So you set up a crowdfunding campaign at a site like Indiegogo.com – Aside from being an affiliate partner, the company is a great group of people.

If successful, your crowdfunding campaign will allow you to raise money—but as an important ancillary benefit, your campaign will also allow you to test your movie concept with a built-in, responsive focus group. Assuming you reach your funding goal, you will not only generate your initial buzz, but you will also source the early adopters for your movie. And these early adopters will grow into a group of fans who will help you spread the word about your movie.

Depending on the scope and scale of your movie, once you have successfully completed a crowdfunding campaign, you may choose to leverage this success to seek out traditional investors. But instead of having an untested movie idea, you have a little POC. What's POC? Proof of concept. I credit writer Craig Spector for teaching me about the importance of POC.

At the time of writing, in the United States, President Obama approved a new securities regulation that could potentially allow filmmakers to use Crowdfunding to offer shares of ownership in movie projects. It is still too soon to tell what the ripple effects of this will mean for independent producers. But like all concepts in this book – we are on the brink of some exciting changes!

Regardless of how the laws change, as a tool and model, Crowdfunding helps you prove your concept, source and potentially accelerate the growth of your audience. In the unfortunate event your campaign is not successful, this knowledge will help you go back to the basics and refine your concept before you take the giant leap.

Another Way to Get Money

As I mentioned previously, the name of the game in your first feature is to cut the need for hard cash, while at the same time preserving or improving your production value. In other words, you want to make your movie look more expensive than it is. I also mentioned how some filmmakers employ bartering or trading to get the necessary resources.

While cutting your budget and exchanging cash for favors will involve a lot of creativity and planning, if you can learn to cut costs and be creative with virtually no money, imagine what you will accomplish when you actually have money! A lesser known, yet very popular, way some filmmakers get money to make their movie is called the risk share method.

With the risk share method, you simply ask folks working above the line on your movie if they would like to partner up and throw in some cash. Now, what I'm referring to is VERY RISKY. By risky, I mean the downside to this type of business has to do primarily with liability.

You will need to work with an attorney to structure your business properly so that each person understands their personal risk; otherwise, you could end up liable for everything. The other downside is you could have too many people who think they are a boss of the project, and sometimes this just creates confusion.

If you go into business this way, and you fail to establish your project based on the advice of tax and legal professionals, you could find yourself in a lot of legal trouble. So, as usual...TALK WITH QUALIFIED LEGAL AND TAX PROFESSIONALS BEFORE STARTING! All of this being said, assuming you do your homework and figure out how to structure your movie business the proper way, having the cash contribution of five to 20 people can really add up. And whoever contributes cash will have a vested interest in making the project a success.

Chapter Four

Manufacture Your Movie

"History is more or less bunk. It's tradition. We don't want tradition. We want to live in the present and the only history that is worth a tinker's damn is the history we make today."

–Henry Ford

Assuming you do the work, you will eventually have a great feature screenplay, a breakdown, schedule and a workable budget. But as every movie producer knows, a whole lot can change between development and pre-production. Assuming you can get the cash and an entire team of professionals eager to help you, it's time for the real work! What does this mean?

Take your initial schedule and breakdown, then get ready to modify it. When you have all the filmmaking stuff you need, you're no longer operating from theory and planning. You are now in action mode! At this stage you need to review and modify your initial, ideal schedule for the real-world realities of production. This means you'll need to pick your shoot dates and call times. You'll have to adjust your schedule for locations, cast and crew call times, and general availability. You'll need to plan for weather conditions.

It is at this point in the process when most filmmakers realize that there are many variables. And if you fail to stay on top of your variables, you run the risk of losing momentum and potentially having your entire project fall apart. So you have some thinking to do. And assuming you have found an experienced 1st AD or line producer to work with, you will be able to combine ideas and figure out the best game plan.

Remember, your schedule and your budget are related. Add another day and your costs compound. Subtract a day and you save money. Any changes to the schedule change the budget. Figure out when you can begin production. The time of the year will have an impact on your budget. Hot weather will require different provisions than cold weather. And how will rain impact your shooting schedule? Do you have a Plan B? How about a Plan C? Don't forget food for the cast and crew!

Once you set a shoot date, then it is showtime! You need to check and recheck your equipment, calendar, actors, and crew to make sure everything is proceeding as planned. This is both an exciting time—and a time of high stress. I have been on more than one project where I witnessed people crying. These were not tears of joy.

The important thing to remember is that you aren't doing brain surgery. So if you make a mistake in the process, move on and do things better. If you aren't having fun, even on a bad day, what the heck are you doing?

In order to get your movie project off the ground, you will need a Plan A, B and C. To do this, you need to assemble and enlist the collaboration of an experienced team. This is an area where many filmmakers fall flat on their faces and fail. The reason for these failures is often based on a lack of experience. It is very challenging to anticipate all of your production needs unless you've made a few features. And even then, mistakes are just part of the process.

If you have never made a feature, don't worry. One of the easiest ways to avoid common pitfalls is to put together a team of talented filmmaking collaborators. I have already mentioned the importance of employing a seasoned first assistant director and a line producer. But there are quite a few other folks you must include in your production to make things run smoothly.

Create a Plan B

Here's how it happens. Months in advance, you plan everything for your movie. You get locations, picture vehicles, actor contracts, crew and stunt professionals. And then for some reason, two days before you begin production, crazy events spring up and suddenly locations fall apart, picture vehicles disappear, actors quit the project, and crew members take other jobs that pay more.

If you can maintain a good attitude and roll with these kinds of setbacks, you'll soon find it's just another day in paradise. That being said, you can eliminate a lot of frustration if you prepare for these unexpected events in advance (just in case). Once you have everything locked down, you'll need to compile a PLAN B. No matter how careful you plan, in low-budget movie production, whatever could go wrong, will go wrong! It's your job to plan for it.

If you follow the previous instructions, you've probably figured out how to maintain a high production value with limited cash. Create backup locations (just in case). And while you're planning, make sure you talk with some insurance professionals and a qualified attorney regarding legal protection. I don't meant to sound paranoid, but you can never be too careful!

Get Legal Releases

In addition to working with a lawyer for your location release, you'll want to make sure you have legal releases for everyone associated with your project. Check out filmmakingstuff.com for some release resources. Also, since you're probably hard up for cash, check with your state. Most states have lawyers who can help you with your artistic legal needs at a discount. Determination is usually based on your income.

From my experience, the name of the game is CYA (Cover Your Ass). You will want a release from everyone working on your movie, including the guy cooking the food. You'll also want a release from the actors as well as the location owners. Should any corporate logos make their way into your movie, you will need permission from the corporation. If you're getting music for your film, make sure ALL copyright holders sign on the dotted line, not just the singer!

The other thing you'll want is some production insurance for your movie. Liability insurance will help in the event someone gets hurt on set. There are also people who recommend you consider Errors and Omissions insurance even in preproduction. For more information on the types of insurance you will need to make connections on the online filmmaking forums.

Find a Director

At this point, you should know what you like and dislike about the filmmaking process. If you want to direct your feature, your short movies will have provided you with the experience and confidence to do so. In the event you don't want to direct, that is OK. Since you've been building your network from day one, just go to whatever social networking site is popular and seek out a director with your sensibilities.

If the director has more experience than what you're used to, make a pitch. I mean, the worst thing that can happen is that the director says no. Just know, if you do bring on an outside director, the movie becomes the director's show once production commences. Good or bad, your job is to support the director and make his or her life easier. If this doesn't feel right to you, then it's probably a good indication you should direct your first feature yourself.

Attaching Actors

As you're starting out, you may not be able to get any movie stars to act in your first feature. But you may be able to make up for this shortcoming creatively. Assuming you write a feature with a high concept and a controversial hook, you may have a pretty good chance of building some buzz. And if you have the buzz, you don't have to lose quite as much sleep over the lack of star talent in your movie.

While I'm thinking about it, I have to warn you: The market is flooded with OK movies; movies that would probably have had a better chance if they actually had a "known" actor in the story. If you have access to someone "known," bringing him or her into your production even for just a minute could represent a boost in the value of your project.

If you are fortunate enough to know name talent, but short on funds, you might be in for a pleasant surprise. Many actors are motivated by the prospect of playing challenging characters more than money. Just know that you may need to make provisions with the unions and guilds in order for unionized actors to take a role in your low-budget feature. Check out sagindie.com for information.

For those of us in Hollywood, finding actors is pretty easy. Craigslist, Actors Access and LAcasting come to mind as some of the most popular websites for finding talent. Not to mention, you could probably audition your neighbors as they walk through the lobby of your apartment building. LA is never short of actors looking for experience. (And if you need a zombie fighting filmmaker...Hint, hint, hint.)

Auditions

As a first-time feature filmmaker, you may not live in Hollywood or have access to talent. If this is your situation, visit the theatre department at your local university and find some student actors looking for experience. The added advantage is that you could have the department set aside a room where you could audition actors for free. This would save you the costs and time associated with renting or borrowing an audition location.

By the end, you would have a pretty good idea if anyone can handle your movie as you envisioned it. If not, go to the next university or community theatre. If you are seeking the support of your community, you can also contact various news agencies and promote the casting of your movie. In smaller markets, news organizations love this stuff.

I was featured in my local newspaper on numerous occasions. Getting coverage only took a couple of phone calls. Once you're in the press, don't be surprised if some professionals contact you. In the days prior to the audition, call the actors and provide them with a time. Also, provide them with some pages of script. Many actors do not give very good cold readings. If you give them time to study the scene, you'll make the audition process better for everyone involved. When the audition day comes, do not cast anyone who shows up late.

The only time you should break this rule is if the actor is smart enough to tell you he was coming from another audition/TV show/movie. If this aspiring actor was late and not smart enough to offer this exact excuse, do not hire him.

Granted, if he is unbelievably good and had an excuse that sounds OK—then maybe take the risk. But if he flakes later, remember that I did warn you.

When you find the actors you want, call them up. Congratulate them. Then invite them to the table read.

The Table Read

Have all the actors over to read the work in one sitting. Make sure you provide food and beverages. If you aren't the writer, make sure you invite them. Then, after you introduce the entire cast to each other, begin the read. As the producer, you may opt to announce the scene headings and action. There may be certain aspects of the script that don't work at all. If this happens, you may want to rewrite or cut the scene. The table read will give life to words. Make sure you take notes.

The Director of Photography

The director of photography is the director's right-hand man. The DP will figure out how best to shoot the movie to capture the tone and story in a way that communicates the director's vision. You should allow the director to pick his or her DP. Since you are shooting a movie on a limited budget, it's great to find a DP who owns equipment and is willing to rent it for a very reasonable price.

In my experience, a low-budget movie offers a creative DP wiggle room for experimentation. Perhaps the DP has a new camera to test. If this is the case, your low-budget movie may offer a great proving ground. I've been involved in low-budget productions in which the DP actually brought in a gaffer and some key members of the crew. When you have an eager director, an enthusiastic DP and a great gaffer, you are on your way to creating a recipe for magic.

Audio

Typically sound wouldn't be included this early in most producers' hierarchy of needs, but experience has taught me audio is one of the biggest oversights. You will need very good sound or your movie will be terrible. So many times sound is overlooked. And by the time the filmmaker figures out he or she has a problem, it's usually in the editing room. And it's too late!

If you did a whole bunch of shorts, I don't need to remind you how important sound is to your production. Working within a low budget, there is no room for audio error. Half of your cast will be working for next to nothing. So if your edit requires additional dialogue recording (ADR), getting your cast back after the wrap will be pretty expensive, if not impossible.

Also, if the actors flake after the shoot, you'll be stuck with a pile of sound garbage. So I suggest finding the best boom operator and a sound mixer and convincing them to work on your movie. If they agree, treat them like gold, because without them, your movie will be in a lot of trouble.

Photos on Set

Aside from bad sound, the other area filmmakers overlook is getting pictures of actors during production. Find a photographer to get on the set. You'll want a whole bunch of high-quality pictures. Some of these will be used for your festival press kit, general publicity and your website. Don't forget this.

Get Crew

So far, if you followed the low-budget guidelines, you've set yourself up for a high-concept, controversial story set in just a few locations carried out by a small number of actors. If all of this is in place, getting your crew should be a breeze. This is when you should call in your line producer or 1st AD.

Traditionally the line producer or production manager manages the cash expenditures and is concerned with the budget, as well as the overall supervision of physical production. If you bring one of these people on from the start, he or she will help you refine your initial breakdown and rework your budget. It has been my experience that having an experienced line producer is invaluable in the prep phase of your movie.

The other essential professional you need is an experienced 1st AD. These hard workers will refine the schedule (again) and then keep the movie on time and on schedule. These two roles are essential. Once you have these folks in place, they will provide you with guidelines on how to hire the crew.

The easiest way to find a crew is through referrals, especially in the movie industry. People trust people they've worked with in the past. So go into your network and find out who knows whom. In the event you fall short in this area, simply put an ad on Craigslist or Mandy.com, and you'll be able to find a crew pretty easily. More than likely, you'll want a wardrobe person and another person to coordinate the food. You'll want to have a couple of production assistants on hand to fill in as needed.

Once you have some help, make sure everyone's needs are being met. Talk with the sound people, the camera people and the director to hear their ideas. Once you get into the groove, you'll find most people get very creative in a small cast and crew production.

A couple of years ago, we did a 35mm TV commercial with a crew of seven. Each of us was cross-trained to handle multiple jobs. When we got onto the set, each carried out every task with professionalism. I include this to say that even if you're short in terms of cash and crew with limited locations, as long as you utilize creativity, you can make due.

Food Is Finance

A couple days before production, drive to the nearby wholesale mart and load your trunk up with goodies. People like food on set. And when everyone is working on a budget, you should know that food is the most essential fuel for everyone. DO NOT GO GENERIC. Buy the best. I'm serious.

If someone wants Oreos, get the real thing, not some fake imitation. If your food is subpar, everybody's attitudes will suffer. If attitudes suffer, your movie will suffer. Now I know this is your first feature, but trust me on this. And in case you think pizza will suffice, think again. Pizza will only work for one meal! After that your cast and crew need variety.

If you haven't already done so, you need to find someone willing to cook for the shoot. Like the director's shot list, each meal should be planned out well in advance. Your cook should enjoy cooking and bring a flair of creativity to the meals. The meals should be light and nourishing, and the appearance should resemble a catered affair. There should be a table overflowing with delicious snacks.

Lock Your Locations

Getting locations can be arduous or easy. It's up to you. In LA, everyone knows they can make money on locations, so finding places to shoot your movie becomes increasingly expensive. However, if you shoot somewhere outside of LA, the price goes down dramatically. I recommend checking in with your state film office. In addition to offering resources like locations, they will also detail film tax credits.

One of the easiest ways to find locations is to go out and scout them. Go into the field with a list of potential spots and drive around with a digital camera. Take pictures. Work to find a location that may fit your movie

You'll want to find out who owns the property you are interested in filming on and get full contact information. Then, when you speak with the owner, describe the scope of your project and tell this person you're shooting a movie. Ask how much it would cost to shoot on the property. Outside of the big cities, this cost is usually minimal. In the event you will have lots of local press coverage, you may find that some business owners are willing to let you shoot for free in exchange for the inherent publicity.

If the owner of the business agrees to let you utilize the property, then you should present a legal release that grants you permission to film on the property. If you speak with a lawyer (or conduct a web search), you will find standard examples of releases for filmmakers.

Obviously, you should still get an attorney to look over the release and make sure it's OK. And later, when you submit the release to the owner, allow him or her a couple days to read it over. When you finalize the location and the shoot dates, establish a Plan B location. If you lose the location, you'll have a nice fall back option.

Befriend the Press

If you are shooting a feature film, you can announce your project through The Hollywood Reporter and Variety. This notification will then be posted as a little blurb in the industry trades. Just go to The Hollywood Reporter website to find instructions on how to submit your production information. Assuming you meet all the requirements, you will then see your project listed with other, big-budget movies.

Once your production is posted, you will get calls from vendors trying to sell you stuff, as well as potential distributors wanting a first look. Do not get overly excited. Distributor solicitation at this stage doesn't necessarily mean you have a deal in the works. These distributors are doing their job and simply seeking out new material. They contact almost every indie production announced in the trades. When you get the calls, simply take down the contact information. You can research the company later. If these folks have a good track record, you can consider them as a potential distributor. But in this stage of the game, you must continually focus on making a good movie.

Publicity is great. Especially when it's free. And especially when the publicity is international. And especially when the publicity drives traffic to your movie website — traffic you can then convert to cash. When we produced our first zombie movie, we had the great fortune of being profiled in a national entertainment magazine. In fact, once the magazine hit the stands, so many people flooded our website that our server went bonkers. This taught us the value of publicity.

Getting publicity for movies in Hollywood is made easier when you have a few movie stars attached to your project. Although getting "name" actors in your movie may not be a reality for you, there are still simple ways to get your project noticed.

You'll need to present your project as newsworthy and cool if you hope to attract press attention. This will come from having a strong story hook, and this is super important. You will want to craft a pitch specific to relevant publications. Publications want content of interest to their audience. Content attracts targeted readers and subscribers. Readers and subscribers attract advertising. Advertising pays for the publication.

Keep this in mind whenever you make your pitch!

When trying to promote a movie that folks have otherwise not heard of, you want as much publicity as you can get. And in this regard, even if you're producing your movie somewhere locally, you need to make sure you present your marketing message with consistency. I share this because, regardless of publication or geography, most anything written about your movie will end up on the Internet. So you need to always be mindful of how you present your project.

In other words, as the press comes around, make sure the story you share with the public is always consistent with previous stories. As a smart marketer, you'll want to create your story right from the start. Depending on the publication, a common theme of interest will be how you and your production team overcame obstacles.

If you plan on producing your movie outside of major film cities like LA and NYC, then getting the attention of local press might be pretty simple. In these areas, you might even attract attention for a short movie. Why is this important? Because you will want to keep an ongoing collection of all good press written about you and your movie projects.

Production

Production is a result of months and months of planning and preparation. I'll repeat again. When making a movie, production is the result of months and months of planning. I emphasize the planning aspects of pre-production, because many filmmakers crash and burn during production because they didn't have a solid plan.

But you're different. To make sure your production goals are executed in such a way that you get the most movie for your hard earned money, you will need to check and recheck with your department heads to make sure everything is A-Okay. Assuming you have a Plan A, Plan B and Plan C, you're ready!

If you're directing, work with your director of photography to get an assortment of cutaways. You'll need many cutaway options to save you from yourself, should you miss something in post-production. I'm not kidding.

Again, work with a great first assistant director. You see that I emphasize this a lot. This is because a seasoned 1st AD can save your show. And while you're at it, hire a bunch of production assistants to help make your life easier! This is an area that I haven't talked about too much. But a good PA is like a good athlete. They can keep momentum.

The production process is a ton of fun. You'll bond with other creative folks and by the end, assuming that all goes well, you and your crew will feel like family. It doesn't matter if you're directing or producing.

Get Some Sleep

This is the best piece of advice I was ever given. The night before your first day of production will be a time of energy, nerves and, if you don't relax, insomnia. Do everything you can to avoid the tossing and turning and get some sleep.

In the morning, drive to the location before everyone else. You won't always do this. But for your first feature, go into the location and take a couple minutes to sit down in a quiet spot. Then take a deep breath and mentally picture yourself making the movie and having the greatest time of your life. After that, picture yourself in the edit room watching the early stages of your movie.

Envision yourself showing your work to friends and family and screening it in front of appreciative audiences. Picture the movie becoming a national sensation or a cult hit. Picture your phone ringing off the hook with producers and managers and agents from Hollywood inviting you to dinner. Get a mental picture of your upcoming success. I could go on...

But now isn't the time. You have a movie to make. So get off your ass and review the day's schedule. Your crew will be first on set and will immediately begin setting up the first shot. When they arrive, make sure the food is ready. Remember, on a low-to-no-budget production, food is the most important asset.

Actors will arrive next. Hopefully, they will be relaxed and prepared to give the best performances of their careers. But if experience has taught me anything, amateurs, inexperienced actors and friends-as-actors require managed expectations. If you can do it, while the crew is setting up, have the actors take their places and rehearse the scene with script in hand.

In the event things look bad, do the best you can to adapt to ever-changing circumstances. If you have to, shoot one line. Call cut. Let the actors practice the next line. Shoot. Call cut. Practice the next line. Shoot. Call cut. You'll do this all day, checking each shot off your list.

At the end of the day, record 30 seconds of ambient noise with everyone in their places. You'll need this if you have to cut airplane noise or loop dialogue.

Your time on the set can be long. If you fall behind, your days can become longer. Long days with little rest and lots of work can cause stress. Don't be surprised if you hit the wall from time to time and break down. Most people either lose their temper or cry or both. If you have to cry or lose your temper, call a time out and take a walk. Go somewhere nobody can see you. There is no quicker way to lose credibility than losing your emotions on the set — especially a low-budget set.

In addition to this, don't forget: You're not alone. Assuming you did a good job planning your days and your shots, you can rest assured everyone is working alongside you to do the best job they can. Once you build momentum during production, assuming you meticulously planned everything, you'll soon find that most everyone working on the movie will fall into a collective, collaborative groove. Getting into the rhythm of production is an awesome feeling! It's one of the major reasons we do what we do.

Even when everything is going as planned, you still need to make sure you pay attention to the little things. For example, I met with one producer who told me how props were sure wardrobe would bring the watch...And wardrobe was sure props would bring the watch. When it came time for the shot, nobody had the watch.

This minor boo-boo resulted in overtime and meal penalties for more than 30 people. These minor hiccups can have not-so-minor consequences. One too many of these overlooked elements can hurt the morale on the set, slow down production, and hurt the final product. To keep your production running smoothly, you'll need to create a shot list, shoot numerous cutaways, record great sound, have awesome FOOD and get all necessary legal releases!

Everyone wants to make the best movie possible. And for the reminder of the shoot, these people will be your family and share lifetime memories with you. If you move at a good pace, while working to have fun, you will eventually yell:

"That's a Wrap!"

Wrap Party

As I get older, I'm not always impressed with nights out on the town. First of all, when I drink, I have a tendency to say and do stupid stuff. These antics were fine in college, but more and more, I realize drinking is incongruent with living my ideal life.

Working as a professional in Hollywood means everyone knows everyone. So you never know whom you'll bump into. It's good to stay sharp.

That being said, I think people can let their guard down and enjoy themselves guilt free after making a movie. The movie-making process is stressful. A couple cocktails to celebrate with cast and crew is a nice way to officially end the production. But even with the movie in the can, do me a favor: Don't do anything stupid. Please do not drink and drive. But you probably KNOW that.

I will add one more tip: Avoid sleeping with somebody from the cast or crew. Trust me on this!

Edit Your Movie

Editing your movie is the final rewrite of your film. This is the time when you add all sorts of amazing layers to your work and smooth out the rough edges and finally complete the picture. Because you've had all that experience with shorts, editing should be no mystery. The difference now is thinking in terms of a longer story. Most likely you have tons of footage from your shoot. Now it's just a matter of getting it onto your computer and assembling it in a way that makes your work enjoyable. But unlike production, you are now faced with the art of throwing some footage in the trash.

Actually, since you're working on a computer, you won't really throw unused footage in the trash. However, you most likely won't use it. Make sure you get every shot and all of your actor dialogue into the computer and then into the timeline. Take a look at all your shots. Take the best ones and put them onto your computer. Once you select your shots, put them on your timeline and cut away.

When you reach this point in the filmmaking process, prepare to sit for hours in a dark edit suite. Now, even if you've edited your previous shorts, with a feature you might consider getting a second set of eyes in the edit suite. I prefer to work with an editor and then provide loose notes. I have some filmmaker buddies who prefer to cut the movie themselves. Either way, the editing process will provide you a perfect opportunity to lose yourself in the rhythm of your movie.

You're going to cut some scenes out. Scenes that you thought were minor will become pivotal to your story. You're going to add music and sound FX and clean up any rough actor dialogue. You will design, and you will refine.

Once you get a rough cut, have some friends watch it. After their feedback, cut the fat. Keep the scenes that work. Repeat this process as necessary, and after many hours, you will finally have something slightly resembling your initial idea. Screen your movie with people who have never seen the movie. Get their reactions and find out what you need to tweak. This is your rough cut.

Like writing a screenplay, everything in the final cut of your movie should be in line with the overall picture. If anything slows down the story, it needs to go. And if you want to be successful in the movies, you'll need to learn how to let go. Otherwise you'll bore your audience and get rejected by every film festival and then wonder why. I don't want that for you.

Once you have what you think is the final cut, take a vacation. Give yourself a week or two where you don't watch your movie at all. During this time, distract yourself with other projects. Don't fall into the tweaking trap. Otherwise, you'll lose perspective. Your work will suffer. You'll waste time. I know it from experience…Trust me.

Get Music

One major component to any great movie is great music. In Los Angeles, there are many up-and-coming, talented bands that will happily sign rights to let you utilize a song or two in your movie. But if you don't live in LA, fear not. This is a time when you can network with bands via social networking sites. When you find someone you like, just write an email:

```
Dear Cool Band,

My name is Jason Brubaker. I'm producing my
first feature. I really like your music and
wonder what it would take to utilize it in my
movie. Could you please provide some details?
Also, please keep in mind we are operating
with a micro budget. So if you require large
payments, we may not be a good fit. But again,
I like your work and welcome the opportunity
to chat.

Sincerely,

Jason Brubaker
```

If you hear no response, move on to the next band. Like most things, bold persistence in the face of rejection is rewarded. Just know that acquiring music rights can be very complicated. So please speak with an experienced professional or legal advisor before using someone else's music in your movie.

After Your Vacation

Invite people who have never seen your movie to come over for a screening. Put the movie on the TV and watch it. Give everyone a notebook so they can write down their thoughts. When the movie ends, have a discussion. Find out what worked and what didn't. Listen very closely for similar notes. As a rule, if more than one person notices the same thing, it could potentially reveal a problem area. If you agree, fix it in your next pass.

Once you get all the feedback, go back to the cutting room. Retweak the movie based on the notes with which you agree. Ignore the notes with which you don't. Then have another screening with a different group of friends. You'll hear other opinions. If you ignored any opinions that are consistent with the first test screening, you're obviously being pompous. So go back and fix the problem. Most likely, by the second test screening, it should be a pretty smooth experience.

Go back and make your tweaks. Once you complete them, you're pretty much done. Congratulations. You are now in the feature club!

Chapter Five

Marketing and Distribution

"I always wanted to see if I could sell a movie to the public without doing any marketing because my philosophy was like, hey man, I'm reaching my audience every day. I'm twittering with them. I'm in direct contact with them on the podcast."

–Kevin Smith

In years past, filmmakers only self-distributed their movies when they had to. It wasn't a choice! But deteriorating DVD sales channels coupled with new advances in digital distribution have changed the game. YOU now have amazing opportunities to make movies reach your audiences and collect cash without the middleman. As a result of this evolution, you need to start thinking about your movie business like any other small business. YOU will create a product. YOU will distribute your product. YOU will market your product. YOU will sell your product. While this seems easy for some modern moviemakers, what I am suggesting represents a total paradigm shift.

Like many first-time filmmakers, our first feature was met with empty distribution promises and crappy deals. So by necessity, we started selling our title on the Internet as both a physical DVD and a video on demand download. At first, none of the producers liked that idea. I mean, even if a traditional deal is terrible, at least there is still validation in seeing your title on the shelves at the local video store.

But then we made our first sale. We thought it was an anomaly. How could we possibly make money with our movie? We had no movie stars, our production values left a lot to be desired, and most people had never heard of our title. But then we made another sale. And a third. And then a dozen…

That was 2006 and, since that time, my enthusiasm for video on demand distribution has only increased. These days filmmakers have a countless options for reaching their audience, creating community, and building buzz. As your own VOD distributor, you can finally get your title seen and selling without waiting for some middleman to give you permission. Assuming you have all the necessary legal documents, releases, and errors and omissions insurance for your movie, the following strategies will help get your movie seen and selling.

Film Festival Marketing

Independent moviemaking has changed forever. In the old days, filmmakers would make a movie and cross their fingers. They hoped to get into Sundance and win a major studio deal and cash advance. While I will always encourage you to think big, if you are basing your movie business on the Sundance dream, you are making a BIG mistake.

Why? Out of the nearly 10,000 films produced each year, only a very small percentage of titles make it into Sundance. And out of those that do make it, only a few garner a traditional distribution deal worth writing about.

With that said, I still think festivals are relevant. Festivals provide you with a good way to get your movie in front of a live audience. And because regional festivals are newsworthy, if you are savvy and aggressive, you can probably get your movie mentioned by various regional press junkets. Even if there is no shot at winning one of those awesome, ground-breaking, dream distribution deals, sharing the experience with the independent film community is always exciting.

I remember one of our earliest festivals. We were invited to some private party in a fancy hotel in Hollywood. There were a few celebrities and respected indie filmmakers milling about. But what was really odd was the fact that most of the festival staff approached me in an overly friendly way. What I didn't realize was that our movie was slated to win an award!

The next night, we arrived on the Fox Studio Lot for the award ceremony. I can remember how exciting it was when they called my name, and I walked down the aisle with flash bulbs exploding in my face. The experience was totally surreal and amazing. After our win, my team and I hit the ground running. We had a two-week open door to submit our spec material to various agents and managers.

For weeks and weeks, I waited for the studios to call with a major deal. But the deal never came. In fact the only thing I got out of the experience, aside from having my ego stroked, was the realization that it was going to take much more than a festival win to garner Hollywood fame and fortune. It was a tough lesson to learn, but valuable. Since then, I have been to many film festivals. And over time, I have realized that most festivals are populated by filmmakers eagerly advertising their screening times to other filmmakers. As a silver lining, sometimes film festivals provide free beer.

While having delusions of distribution grandeur is still part of the film festival fun, with the demise of DVD distribution, it is vitally important that you create a film festival strategy PLAN B. What is a film festival strategy PLAN B? Simply put, if you are serious about making your movie profitable, YOU are now responsible for marketing, promotion and distribution of your movie. And in line with this strategy, you must view regional and second-tier festivals as an opportunity to build your audience list. But instead of handing out postcards to other filmmakers, your marketing strategy will be smarter.

Before you hop on an airplane, write a press release targeted to the specific festival and then distribute your release to the local press. Part of this strategy also involves picking up the phone and personally inviting the press to attend your screening. Many festivals will have a press list. You can use the list they give you, but I would also advise conducting additional Internet searches for other local press outlets.

In addition to the regional media, many towns have a filmmaker community. Reach out to the communities via Facebook or other social networking hubs. Make friends. If you are traveling, it is great to meet up someone to pal around with and share a few drinks. The secondary benefit to this is that many of these same people will have relationships with the festival staff. It is always good to know people on the staff.

On the day of your screening, take several clipboards into your screening if the festival allows it. You will want to collect the names and email addresses of each viewer and get their permission to add them to your email list. The most important strategy for your modern moviemaking career is to grow your own fan base.

Sharpen Your Hook

If you followed the tips earlier in this book, you already have an understanding of your target audience, and you are now ready to enter into the distribution phase of your moviemaking process. Whenever I speak at film workshops and festivals about modern movie distribution, I am often asked if filmmakers should still consider finding a traditional theatrical or DVD distribution deal. My answer to this question is simple. If you are fortunate enough to land an offer that makes sense, take the offer! The problem is that most traditional movie distribution offers are fairly worthless.

Most filmmakers do not find this out until the festivals are over, and all promotional money has been exhausted. This is usually the time when I get phone calls from frantic filmmakers seeking marketing help. At the same time, many of them believe they have created the most amazing movie on earth and cannot understand why nobody has "bought it." While I cannot speak for traditional acquisitions executives, I can tell you two things that I see a lot with independent movies:

1. The movie has niche audience potential, but does not clearly communicate to the appropriate audience.
2. The movie does not have a clearly definable niche audience, which means both the filmmaker and the marketing targets everybody with two eyeballs and a pulse.

Out of both of these scenarios, the easier one is defining the appropriate niche. Depending on how you pronounce the word, niche rhymes with rich. And I firmly believe that niches will make you riches. When filmmakers hire me for a consultation, we discuss various movie marketing strategies, both online and offline. We work to sharpen the movie marketing hook and figure out the most cost-effective ways to redefine and reach the appropriate target audience.

A good client is someone who has crunched numbers and has realistic expectations on how much money the movie can potentially recoup and how long this will take. Unfortunately many filmmakers have not read this book. As a result, they fail to think in terms of their defined target audience. As a marketing rule, attempting to target everybody is the same as targeting nobody. Think about it. You don't have enough money to target everybody. But you should have enough money to cover the cost of entry into the video on demand marketplace.

The VOD Aggregator

Even with non-discriminatory distribution, many straight to DVD distributors are jumping into the video on demand marketplace with a predatory mindset. But this time, instead of promising to get your movie into the video store, these companies now offer you the opportunity to get your movies into popular marketplaces like iTunes. The big difference between VOD and DVD is that you also have the ability to enter the VOD marketplace without utilizing a middleman.

In the event a traditional distributor approaches you touting the wonders of iTunes, you can be very selective. Without an upfront advance, you will need to determine if there is any value in the deal. And while the idea of non-discriminatory distribution is awesome, I am not the only filmmaker in the world who knows this. Filmmakers have saturated the marketplace with content, which creates a ton of competition.

Your job from this point forward is to view your independent moviemaking business just like any other business. You must find your customers (your audience) and create a growing list of people who know you and know your work. There are several ways to make this happen.

As mentioned earlier in this book, your first step is to determine your unique selling proposition, or USP, for each movie you make. What is your movie about? What makes your movie distinguishable from all the other movies in the marketplace? Why would your audience want to see your movie? By revisiting these questions now, you can revisit, tweak, test and refine your marketing message to help you determine which marketplaces are most appropriate for your types of movies and the niche target audience you are trying to attract.

Enter the Marketplace

After a run at the festivals, you will need to determine the appropriate video on demand marketplace for your movie. There are many options for this, including setting up your own Internet storefront, joining other filmmakers in a shared storefront or setting up shop in popular video on demand marketplaces. Since most VOD outlets do not require an exclusive deal, I recommend getting your movie into multiple markets. My preference leans toward iTunes, Amazon and Hulu.

To access these marketplaces quickly, research a company called Distribber at MovieSalesTool.com. I first found the service when I was looking for an easy way to get my movies seen and selling. I liked the service so much that we have worked out an affiliate deal. (This means Distribber pays me to promote. So conduct your own due diligence prior to purchasing any services.) And in addition to this, I have also worked for Distribber, serving as the Director of Operations. So obviously, I am biased. But these relationships were a result of my initial enthusiasm and belief in the company. Let me explain…

The reason I like the service is that, for a one-time upfront fee (and a $79, yearly maintenance fee), Distribber offers filmmakers a non-exclusive deal and the ability to get their movies into iTunes, Hulu and quite a few other popular video on demand marketplaces. Once your title goes live, your sales across all platforms will be managed in one place.

In addition to iTunes and Hulu, Distribber allows you to get your movie seen and selling in many other popular VOD marketplaces as well. And because Distribber stays current with emerging VOD marketplaces, this list is growing. For example, if some new video on demand platform emerges, you can rest assured that the Distribber folks are already out there, working to make the pipeline available to filmmakers.

But the best part is compensation. Unlike deals with a traditional distribution company, Distribber is transparent. While others take a huge chunk of your ongoing, back-end profits, Distribber merely charges a one-time, upfront fee. Once in the system, filmmakers then able get paid on their earnings from all market pipelines. Additionally, filmmakers are not locked into some outrageous, exclusive contract. So if the day comes that you want out, you can get out!

While Distribber can help you access a number of VOD platforms, it is important to note that each marketplace has different submission requirements. For example, aside from having a good movie, some markets require that the filmmaker has errors and omissions insurance. Other markets, like iTunes are very discriminatory. So in the event your title is not selected for a market, Distribber will refund your investment, minus $39.

One of the most exciting outlets to emerge on the indie scene is Hulu. Unlike some of the other marketplaces, Hulu runs on advertising revenue. With this model, a viewer does not need to pull out their wallet and enter credit card information to access your movie. Instead, a viewer can simply find your movie and watch it without obstacles.

To get your movie onto Hulu, revisit Distribber and sign up for the Hulu service. Assuming your movie is accepted, I would advise embedding your movie's Hulu code right onto your website. Once complete, if your website visitor stays long enough to watch an advertisement, then Hulu will share a percentage of the advertising revenue with you. This means you can potentially make money even if people don't stick around to watch your entire movie.

Some moviemakers find the upfront fee can be a barrier to entry. If that is your situation, you are in luck. At the time of writing, Distribber is owned by the popular crowdfunding company Indiegogo. As a result of this relationship, filmmakers are encouraged to create crowdfunding campaigns to cover their Distribber fees. Creating an Indiegogo crowdfunding campaign will not only help you cover the costs necessary to access the various VOD marketplaces, but you will also benefit from the social networking aspects of the site.

Assuming you have great Internet traffic, you may also consider streaming your movie on your website. There are several website embeddable players that have gained popularity within the filmmaking community, such as Dynamo Player (dynamoplayer.com), Distrify (distrify.com) and a company called WatchBox (thewatchbox.com). Some of these tools go beyond just streaming and actually allow the filmmaker to create affiliate promotions. These affiliate add-ons provide enthusiastic movie fans with an additional incentive to share a favorite title with their social networks.

Create Your Movie Sales Funnel

Most Internet businesses are built on something called a sales funnel, or conversion funnel. I credit the famous Internet marketer Fred Gleeck for introducing me to this concept. The sales funnel idea simply means that if you are trying to sell a product or a service on the Internet, you must view your website like a funnel. Targeted prospects enter the top of the funnel and sales come out of the bottom. Since not everybody who visits your movie website will buy your movie, it is essential that you drive more and more targeted visitors to your movie website and "funnel" them to a purchase.

If you are utilizing the Filmmaker Theme for WordPress found at IndieMovieSite.com, your site is already optimized for "funneling" traffic toward a sale. But in the event you are modifying your website, you can begin funneling traffic simply by removing all distracting content from your site, including production photos, press kits and actor bios. Once these items are removed, emphasis should be placed on your trailer, your "about" page and, importantly, your "buy now" buttons.

Even with the best funnel on earth, most of your visitors will exit your website and never return. So to increase your odds of converting these visitors into paying customers, you will want to create ways to capture visitor contact information. One easy way is by creating a Facebook page for your movie and then placing a prominent Facebook link on your site. In this way, filmmakers can connect with you and other fans in your online community. This provides some added social proof that your movie is indeed, awesome.

As mentioned earlier in this book, your audience is your business. Without an audience, you have no business. So as a primary objective, migrate your fans off the social networking sites and get them into an email mailing list that you manage. As mentioned earlier, for this I recommend using the reputable third-party email marketing service AWeber. Again, you can look them up via my affiliate link at AudienceList.com. This is the same service I utilize to manage my own email-marketing and mailing lists. In full disclosure, the company does pay me to promote, but I have been using the service for years and I could not imagine running my business without this tool.

As a rule of thumb, you never want to manage your email marketing campaigns from your own servers. Always use a third-party email marketing company that insists on something called a double opt-in. A double opt-in means that after people submit their name and email to your list, they will still need to check their email for a confirmation link. Then in each subsequent email you send out to your list, you will always provide an easy way for your subscribers to opt-out, or unsubscribe.

With AWeber, as soon as you sign up for one of its inexpensive accounts, you can easily create ways for your movie fans to connect with you. In this sense, email marketing works like this: The bigger your list of targeted subscribers, the more sales you can potentially make over the life of your business. I use email marketing for both my filmmaking and my Filmmaking Stuff. For an example of how this works, go to FreeFilmmakingBook.com. When you arrive on the page, you'll see that I ask for your name and email address. The reason I ask is because I want to build a long term relationship with you.

Filmmaker Rory Delaney provides a great example of how this works for his movie Toxic Soup. When you visit Rory's movie website, ToxicSoupMovie.com, you can see that Rory's initial movie website is very streamlined. It involves both a YouTube trailer as well as an opt-in form. This is intentional. The goal of his movie website, aside from selling movies, is to collect names and email addresses of prospective audience members. Later on, in addition to his current movie, Rory will have the ability to promote related products or other movies of a similar genre to his audience.

There is a science to maintaining relationships through email. You need to know your audience. And you need to make sure all of your communication is on point. For example, if you are making a movie about vegetarians, it would not be a good idea to cross-promote hamburgers, unless you were being ironic or looking to alienate your fans.

But if you work hard to manage your audience list, long after your movie has played the festivals and sold out on iTunes, Hulu and Amazon, you may find there is value in promoting other movies of a similar genre to your subscribers. Better yet, you can start promoting your next movie. This is when having a list really pays off, literally. Or as they say in the world of Internet marketing, the money is in your list.

Refine Your Trailer and Promote It

You need a trailer. A trailer is a sales tool used to get people interested in seeing your movie. The mechanics of creating a trailer are not too complicated. Just find some cool footage from your movie and then smash it into a two-minute video. Add music and a deep voice over, and you're good to go, right? Well, not so fast...

Creating a good trailer is very important. But a lot of filmmakers screw this up by telling us the whole movie or by failing to think in terms of the target audience. Again, who are you trying to attract to your movie? An 18-year-old college male who enjoys slasher gore will most likely respond differently than a 30-year-old female searching for a romantic comedy.

Aside from being too general, a lot of filmmakers end up telling the whole movie in two minutes. Please don't do that. The goal of your trailer is to present your audience with just a small taste of your movie so they will want more. In fact, you want your audience to buy your movie. So it is important you don't tell the entire story. Just limit your trailer to simply providing your viewers with a few good clips.

If you are having trouble cutting a trailer, go onto the Internet and find trailers for movies similar to your own. Then use the trailer as a template. Make your scenes the same length. Use similar music. Add a similar deep voice. Once your trailer is complete, post your trailers on popular video sites and see what sticks.

The Internet is full of places where you can upload and post your trailer. But as I mentioned earlier in this book, YouTube is top-notch. Aside from being the second largest search engine on earth, the service also incorporates a built-in social networking component that allows people to comment and discuss your movie and create community around your title. This is important because word-of-mouth indicates what people like and dislike about your movie. And as you will soon learn, more discussion (good or bad) equals more sales.

If you create a good trailer, you will know this because your video view count will increase, and the comments will be favorable. In the event that your viewership is low, determine if your description appeals to your target audience. If not, you will want to tweak and test your description, title and tags to find out if it makes a difference in viewership.

In the event your viewership does not increase, consider re-evaluating your trailer. Is your trailer congruent with your hook and the marketing elements we covered earlier? If not, I suggest you recut and refine your trailer to make sure your marketing message is consistent. More often than not, you can make your trailer more appealing. You simply need to cut your trailer to a shorter length. Once you streamline your trailer, retest and see if your traffic improves. If there is no improvement, then it is possible you are communicating a message that is inconsistent with what your audience wants.

When this happens in big-budget movies, studio marketers will often recut and remarket the trailer to appeal to other target audiences. For example, let us assume that you made an action movie with a love story element. It is possible you could cut a trailer to focus on the love story elements and then position the movie as a love story.

You could also create a trailer that emphasizes the action and then communicate this angle to action-movie enthusiasts. Just keep in mind that repositioning your movie to be something it isn't could be risky. Aside from being deceptive, if you upset your audience, you might get some not-so-good feedback.

One last tip. Because many people will embed your YouTube trailer on their own sites, you will want to close your trailer with a call to action. I suggest something simple like this: Order now. Go to FreeFilmmakingBook.com.

Increase Web Traffic

Assuming you have been following the suggestions in this book, by now you have built an Internet presence that consists of a YouTube channel, a Twitter profile, a Facebook page, an email list and various websites. As a reminder, the reason for all of this work is to expand your footprint, attract and engage your target audience, and eventually make more movie sales.

Because the modern movie going audience is fragmented, targeted Internet traffic is paramount to the success of your title. To increase your website traffic, you might decide to work out Search Engine Optimization tactics with your web marketer, pay for online or off-line advertising, or incorporate a bit of everything. Unpaid traffic is called organic. Organic traffic is the best kind because whenever you pay for a customer, you diminish your profit margin from the outset. So obviously, the goal for all movie marketers is to acquire a customer for the very lowest price possible.

As we discussed earlier in the book, adding a blog to your website can go a long way toward increasing traffic. The best thing about a blog is most of this traffic is free. Remember, with a blog, consistent updates enable you to further engage your target audience. But the more important objective of blogging is to get your site to show up in search results. So in addition to providing your visitors with frequent project updates, you will also want to incorporate articles that profile complementary subjects.

For example, if your movie focuses on polarizing issues like gay marriage or immigration reform, finding blog article ideas is often as easy as completing a few Google searches for current news. In the event your movie is a character-driven piece that focuses on more subtle subjects, you will need to take a hard look at your story and find a few prominent elements that you can amplify. For example, if you were creating a zombie movie, you might focus on zombie news, behind-the-scenes zombie-moviemaking tips and movie screenings. You might also find creative ways to incorporate aspects of your fictional movie into the blog narrative.

One of the movies I worked on is a documentary called Toxic Soup. Directed by Rory-Owen Delaney, the movie details every day, hard-working Americans afflicted by chemical pollution. While the movie broadly fits into the environmental activism genre, there are many micro-niche topics detailed in the movie. One of the most prominent is a term called chemical body burden. By Googling this topic, we were able to easily find other, closely related topics. This gave us something to blog about. In addition, blog content can be used for email blasts.

By blogging consistently on topics related to your movie, your movie website has a chance of getting indexed by search engines. And once your site begins to rank in search results, you will increase the odds of driving more organic traffic to your site any time someone searches for your topic. This increases your odds of getting visitors on your list, which increase your odds of making sales.

In addition to blogging, knowing your niche topics helps you seek out and engage online communities already interested in your niche subject matter. And because your movie is inline with the community's values, getting initial grassroots support is easier than trying to target the world.

Press Releases

In addition to blogging, one secret I utilize to increase traffic is frequent press release submissions through the services offered at PR Web. Years ago, it was advised that you only submitted press releases when you had something newsworthy to share. But these days, in addition to targeting traditional news outlets, most press release submission websites also syndicate your news all over the Internet. Without getting technical, for a very small fee, submitting one press release complete with links to your website can increase your website footprint exponentially.

In addition to frequent press releases, you will also need to research and build a list of at least 100 websites and publications that cater to your target audience. You will then reach out to each website owner and ask if they would be interested in reviewing your movie. Depending on popularity of your target market, you may find that many of your target websites seem less than professional.

If you did your homework, you might find that these questionable sites are managed by some kid in his parent's basement. But what you have to keep in mind is that on the Internet everybody is somebody and any back links that you can get to your website will increase your "Google juice." This helps your site rank better in organic search results and potentially increases unpaid traffic to your site.

Online Advertising

Every marketer loves sourcing, organic free traffic because the cost of acquiring a customer is very low. But the problem is that it often takes search engines a few months to fully index and rank your web pages. As a result, you need to implement a short-term paid advertising strategy. Popular methods for online paid advertising include Pay-Per-Click (PPC) and Cost-Per-Impression.

Pay-Per-Click

With Pay-Per-Click you pay a service provider like Google AdWords to advertise your website in its search results. You effectively reach your target audience because you bid on keywords. For example, I could request that Google advertises one of our movies called Career Courier in the search results every time someone searches for the words "bike movie." If the person searching for a bike movie clicks on my ad, Google charges a fee.

PPC fees vary depending on keyword popularity and competitor bidding for the same keywords. Luckily, you can set spending limits. You can designate how much money you are willing to pay per click and how much you'll spend per day. If your desired keywords are too expensive, you can opt out. At the time of writing, Google, Yahoo! and Microsoft are the heavy hitters. I have had most of my experience with Google, and it is a pretty easy process; however, there is a downside.

Even if you have the most esoteric product on earth, with PPC, a quick keyword search can help you find your prospective customer, somewhere, out there. So that's the good part. The disadvantage is price. Like any ads, the return must outweigh the investment. With PPC, you're in good shape if someone clicks on your ad and actually buys your product. But if they don't buy, you lose whatever you invested in the click.

Cost-Per-Impression

With CPI (sometimes called CPM), your ad is displayed per 1,000 impressions without the guarantee of a click. With this strategy, you pay to have your advertisement placed on a related website. Unlike PPC, the cost you pay-per-impression is determined by web traffic. With CPI, every unique visitor who visits the site is considered an impression.

Let's say you create a documentary about corporate toxic waste and how it is making people sick. You may decide to advertise on an environmentally focused website. If the site utilizes CPI, your advertisement is displayed every time a person visits the site. With CPI, it doesn't matter if the visitor clicks on your ad or not. Like advertising in a newspaper, with CPI, you are paying for exposure. You are hoping the targeted visitors will see your ad and click on it.

The upside to CPI is that it doesn't matter how many people click through to your site. You don't get charged for the clicks.

The disadvantage is that if you don't research your target market, you could advertise on a site seen by 10,000 people who are not at all interested in your movie.

Offline Print Advertising

A print ad is an advertisement in print mediums such as a newspaper, a magazine, newsletter or a flyer. By now, you should know the target audience for your movie. If you decide to invest money in print advertising, simply research various publications that cater to your demographic. If you are working in the horror/gore genre for example, you can design a good print ad and put it in Fangoria or one of the other many popular publications. Once you find a couple of publications, contact your graphic artist friend and offer to pay a couple hundred dollars for ad creation.

With magazine print ads, there are very strict deadlines. If you miss the deadline, it could delay getting your advertisement printed on time, which could slow up your campaign. Contact the appropriate publications and see if you can work out a deal. In many cases, the price you pay for ad space can be negotiated. Once a price is mentioned, ask this question: "Is that the best you can do?" In many cases, the person on the phone is a salesperson. Salespeople can work out deals if it represents the difference between a sale and nothing.

The advantage to print ads is that it is possible people will keep the magazine around or give the magazine to an equally enthusiastic friend, especially if your ad is featured in a well-known publication specific to your demographic. In this regard, print ads can potentially keep on giving.

Monitor Visitor Data

Many filmmakers set up websites, but then fail to monitor and study visitor data. This is a lot like trying to throw darts in the dark. Maybe you hit the target. Maybe you didn't. To easily monitor website data, I suggest having your webmaster install Google Analytics onto your site. Analytics is a free service offered by Google that allows you to monitor your web traffic. Once installed, in addition to getting a visitor traffic count, you will also get detailed information on how long people stay on your site, what pages are visited, and, most importantly, where your visitors exit.

Time on Site

With one of our titles, we noticed that most of our visitors stuck around long enough to watch the trailer. This is a good thing. But the data also exposed a potentially profit draining hole in our funnel. After watching the trailer, a large percentage of our visitors clicked over to our behind the scenes photos and then exited the site. Since our objective was to get a sale, this was a problem. To resolve this, I simply removed the behind the scenes photos. As a result, our visitors progressed through the funnel as planned, and our sales increased.

Keyword Phrases

In addition to monitoring how your visitors navigate your website, you must also monitor how your visitors find your site. With one of our titles, I noticed that most of our visitors found the website by Googling the name of our movie. This data indicated that our word-of-mouth marketing was very strong. When word of mouth is strong, converting targeted visitors into movie sales becomes easier. But this also assumes that people actually want to pay for your movie. Other keyword phrases like "Watch Career Courier Free," revealed that many fans were trying to figure out how to pirate our movie.

Traffic Sources

You need to find out where your traffic is coming from. For our zombie movie, we got lucky. Because the movie was a bit weird and remarkable, we found that many fan websites mentioned the movie, embedded our trailer, and also included backlinks to our site. But what really caught my attention was the popular social bookmarking site called StumbleUpon.com. After crunching the numbers, I realized that most of our traffic and sales came from this site.

Social Bookmarking for Your Movie

In addition to your movie website, there are about many other websites competing for visitors. While Google and other search engines are pretty good at helping people find what they are looking for, search engines are really just sophisticated computers. Sometimes people favor website suggestions from real people, eliminating the need to sort through dozens of results.

Social Bookmarking sites like reddit, digg, Delicious.com and StumbleUpon provide an easy way for people to share and rank links based on personal relevance. And depending on the content of your movie, some social bookmarking sites are effective for movie marketing.

StumbleUpon is a social bookmarking tool that allows people to share interesting websites with their StumbleUpon networks as well as Facebook, Twitter and email contacts. And if someone happens to "stumble upon" your movie website, you have the potential to garner significant traffic! The reason why I am enthusiastic about the site is because our zombie movie got over 100,000 visitors from the service.

But did you know you can actually pay for someone to "stumble upon" your site? It's true. And it's awesome. The StumbleUpon paid discovery service allows you to choose from three advertising service tiers. Each tier provides a different level of audience targeting. The first tier starts at a nickel per stumble. But here is where it gets interesting. Unlike other paid advertising solutions, StumbleUpon allows for exponential, unpaid traffic.

To explain, let's say you want to target someone into horror movies. So you invest a nickel to get that person to "stumble" your website. But then that person shares your site with four of his friends. Guess what? Because your paid stumble resulted in four additional free stumbles, you really only invested one penny per visit (five cents for five visits). Taking this further, let's say these five stumblers each share your site with one friend. Now you got ten visits for a nickel. That is an investment of merely a half-cent per visit!

Assuming these visitors convert to paying customers, then you may figure out a way to make this simple method very profitable for you. Unfortunately, every movie is different. I initially thought this discovery would provide me with the secret ingredient for selling movies. I have since tested this strategy with other movie websites and so far only a small handful of my test sites resulted in significant traffic. The rest just were not interesting enough to warrant exponential stumbles. But it might be worth testing!

Leverage Your Following

While managing your own marketing, sales and distribution may be a departure from the Sundance Dream, staying focused on building a sustainable movie business will go a long way toward allowing you to live happily ever after. And in the event that you get confused about what to do next, repeat after me: "My audience is my business. Without an audience, I have no movie business..."

One of the most important filmmaking strategies you must adopt in this era of modern moviemaking is a long-term perspective. In years past, filmmakers focused on making one movie, selling it, and then moving on to the next movie. While the idea of creating multiple titles over the course of your filmmaking career has not changed, it is now vitally important that you plan a series of movies from day one. The reason for this is simple. You are now solely responsible for the success of your movie business. And to stay in business, you will need to create a profitable library of titles that continually pay you.

To use a real estate business analogy, in years past you built a house and sold it for maximum profit. But these days, given the changes in the real estate market, it makes sense to hold onto the house, rent it out, and collect rent checks every month. This is the difference between capital gains and cash flow. And as an independent filmmaker, the growing demise in DVD sales outlets means that filmmakers must now focus on creating multiple titles and increasing cash flow over time.

As I mentioned previously, creating a highly targeted mailing list is now essential for your success. Thinking long term, the most important component of your movie making success is establishing a loyal following. From a business perspective, the size of your mailing list will provide a solid metric on which to base forward-looking revenue projections. In other words, you can take look at your list and say "2 percent of our followers bought this movie. I wonder how many fans will be interested in my next movie?" But instead of guess work, you can send your followers an email and ask them.

As you grow your community, your fans will begin to know you, know your company, and celebrate your work. And as long as you continue to provide good entertainment, you may eventually reach mass great enough to fund your future movie projects. Imagine how much prospective investors will appreciate your pitch when you already have 100,000 fans eager to buy your next movie?

In the end, the heart and soul of all forms of distribution is finding an audience willing to pay you for your work. Video on demand simply removes the middleman from the process and allows you to connect directly with the people who matter the most: your audience.

Find Other Filmmakers

If both your traffic and your budget are low, search out other filmmakers who have successfully sold their movies to a similar market and find out if they would be interested in promoting your movie to their mailing list. Assuming your movie is congruent with what their audience enjoys, these other filmmakers may gladly help you out for a cut of the profits. I have found that giving affiliates a good return for effective marketing creates long-term, win-win business relationships. These other filmmakers are able to create a stream of revenue between their movie projects. And you benefit by expanding your movie's reach quickly.

This is also a good time to revisit those sites from your initial research. Compile a list of 100 target websites, then reach out to site owners and kindly ask if they would be interested in reviewing your movie. Regardless of whether or not these folks like your movie, what is secondarily valuable to you are links back to your website. Over time, these back-links, combined with your trailer and social networking profiles, will serve to funnel more prospective viewers back to your website. Some will buy your movie. Some will simply join your mailing list.

And the cycle continues...

Modern Moviemaking Manifesto

1. Modern Moviemakers are entrepreneurs and view each movie as a startup. Instead of raising investment dollars for just one title, Modern Moviemakers focus on creating mini-studios, complete with development, planning, production, marketing, distribution and sales.

2. Modern Moviemakers focus their business on producing a slate of at least five genre specific movies. These movies are created inexpensively and will be delivered to the audience via ALL popular VOD marketplaces.

3. Instead of focusing on projects centered on freelance day-rates, Modern Moviemakers raise enough money to put crew on a salary, with benefits. Everybody in the company will own equity in the company. So in this regard, someone who owns 10% in company stock will get 10% of all movie profits. This will supplement crew salary with an ongoing, lifelong stream of income – and incentivize everybody involved to succeed.

4. Modern Moviemakers work to grow our community (and customer base) bigger. And over time, our fans will begin to know us and celebrate our work. Only in this way will we eventually reach mass great enough to increase ongoing revenue through multiple streams of movie income.

5. Modern Moviemakers believe that producing multiple movie titles over time builds enough buzz to create long term, sustainable revenue. In this regard, modern moviemakers focus on creating entire library instead of just depending on one title to support our career.

Resources

The following resources are my personal picks. While these are the same resources I utilize in my own filmmaking life, in full disclosure, many of these sites pay me to promote. While your price will not be affected, you are encouraged to conduct your own due-diligence prior to making ANY purchases both here and everywhere on earth. With that said...

FreeFilmmakingBook.com provides you and your filmmaking friends with the official filmmaking stuff newsletter as well as several FREE filmmaking resources that you can download.

FilmmakingStuff.com is your professional resource for all of your filmmaking needs. Filmmaking content is updated weekly and the site includes great tips so you can navigate the changing world of filmmaking.

WriteYourMovieNow.com is for writers and screenwriters who want to write movies for the new low budget cinema wave. The site is geared towards first time feature writers and details a step-by-step system for getting your story on paper.

IndieProductionTool.com is an online production management tool that allows you to schedule your movie and manage your production from anywhere.

GetMovieMoney.com is a site devoted to helping filmmakers learn tricks and strategies for contacting and building relationships with prospective investors.

MovieSiteHost.com allows filmmakers to easily get movie site hosting, a domain name and easily set up a WordPress blog website to promote both a movie and a movie company.

MovieScriptBreakDown.com provides online training for filmmakers who want to find out how to breakdown screenplays and schedule their independent movies.

IndieMovieSite.com provides the "Filmmaker Theme" for WordPress. This tool allows you to quickly modify your WordPress site into a movie promotional website.

AudienceList.com allows filmmakers to capture leads from their movie website, build a mailing list, set up email newsletters and a sequential email auto responder.

SellYourMovieNow.com provides tips on getting your finished feature seen and sold. This site contains resources on how to leverage the ever changing world of digital distribution and internet marketing.

MovieSalesTool.com allows you to get your finished feature onto iTunes, Netflix and Amazon.

Movie Making Checklist

☐ Read and study everything you can about the filmmaking process. Also study internet marketing. A good place to start is www.filmmakingstuff.com

☐ Write or acquire a screenplay you want to produce.

☐ Do an initial breakdown, schedule and budget of the project. How much does it cost?

☐ Looking at the initial budget, is there anything you can get for a discount, or free, or barter?

☐ Talk with a lawyer and figure out your best money strategy.

☐ Following the law, go after the money. This will require strategy, persistence and enthusiasm.

☐ This will be one of the tougher parts of the process, but it will make the movie possible.

☐ Most people will want to know how the money is going to be spent, what they can expect in return and how will you eventually get their money back. Filmmaking is a risky business, full of unknowns and you should never sugar coat the potential risk involved in this business.

☐ Have a plan for the movie when it is complete. Will you take the festival route? Will you market it to colleges and universities? Will you send it to sales agents and acquisition pros?

☐ Were you able to get the money? If not, you can choose a new project or alter the screenplay to cut costs.

☐ Get more favors and freebies. Who do you know who has what you need? Remember, if you don't ask, you don't get.

☐ Assuming you did get the money, pick a date for production.

☐ Hire a lawyer to help you with contracts and releases. If you are short on cash, do a web search for lawyers for the arts in your state. If this fails, start cold calling law firms. Maybe you can find someone willing to help you in for ownership (equity).

☐ Try to raise enough money to pay people. If you ask people to work for free, you can expect a lot of "no's" before you find the right fit for your show. Do not let the word "no" stop you!

☐ You can make your job easier if you work with someone with film production experience. However, keep in mind that the more experience someone has, the more you will have to pay.

☐ Finalize your screenplay. Get it to a point where you are not going to keep changing things. Once you get to this point, consider it a locked script.

☐ Number your scenes. Then break down your script, grabbing each element, location and character. Create a schedule.

☐ From your schedule and breakdown, create a final budget. You probably know how much money you have to work with. If you find you don't have enough you have two choices:

    A. Get More Money!
    B. Modify the script and schedule.

☐ Get your crew. I suggest working with a seasoned Physical Producer / Line Producer / Production Manager to help you get organized. These folks will probably look at your schedule and make modifications as necessary.

☐ If you are going to direct and produce, having a 1st AD and Production Manager to help out will open the door to relationships with cast and crew.

☐ The Production Manager will help you hire the right people. They may also know a thing or two about tax credits in your state. This could be invaluable!

☐ I know. Money is tight. So instead of hiring a locations scout, you're going to have to scout and procure locations yourself. This means you will knock on some doors and introduce yourself, your project and your goals.

☐ What can go wrong with a location probably will. So you will want to have a 2nd and 3rd location added to the mix. This way, should something happen, you'll have a fall-back plan.

☐ Assuming you are directing this sucka yourself, you might find a director of photography who shares your sensibilities and has equal enthusiasm for the project.

☐ Your DP will help you design a look and mood for your movie. Given your cost constraints, there is no need to produce your movie with film. You will most likely shoot in HD.

☐ MARKETING: Create a website specific to your movie. Make sure you have a way to get site visitors on your mailing list. I recommend starting an account at www.AudienceList.com (they pay me to promote.) Also have a place for press, so that they can download your press kit and materials.

☐ As you get into production, you will be able to add a movie trailer. (Increase the size of your mailing list and establish a website you can later modify into a sales funnel.)

☐ If you're lucky, you already know some talented actors interested in your project and working with you. You'll have to work out a deal with these folks. LA and NYC offer various websites that help producers find actors.

☐ If you are in rural USA, you might have some difficulty with these options. I suggest partnering with local university drama departments and local theaters to fulfill casting requirements.

☐ Once you have all of your actors, you will want to find a location for a table read. Go through the script. If you wrote it, now is a time to take some notes for a final tweak. Anything changed in the script also changes the budget and the schedule.

☐ Seriously, don't skimp on food. You will want someone in charge of Craft Services. They should be good at going out and getting deals on food and catering. If you cannot find anyone to do this for you, you'll have to do it yourself.

☐ Make sure you have adequate food. If you're doing a union shoot, there are guidelines and rules you must follow. If you're doing a non-union indie, then some advice is: DON'T GET CHEAP! GET QUALITY!

☐ Do you have all of your permits, releases, location agreements? Do you have production insurance? There are so many different types of insurance, it will make your head spin. Make sure you talk with some experienced professionals to make sure you have adequate insurance for your movie.

☐ Meet with your Camera Department and find out how much tape stock you'll need (assuming you're shooting in HD). If you're shooting film, which might be costly for your first feature – you will want to have an idea of these needs too.

☐ Try to take as many naps as you can. This is a fun, but stressful time. So sleep. Exercise. Eat.

☐ Once you have all the above stuff checked off the list, you'll want to meet with your department heads and make sure everyone's needs are being met.

☐ Assuming you have maintained limited locations, with a limited cast and crew, you will probably still be baffled by the amount of questions that come. Be ready to say yes or no!

☐ Seriously, you would think you are making a gazillion dollar movie. But this is indication people care about their work. They care about the movie. And they want to make it a success.

☐ This goes without saying, but don't be a jerk. Seriously, you're making a movie. It's a real accomplishment and it's one of those great things you can do in life. In fact, it's quite awesome. So push forward. ENJOY!

☐ Did I mention you need plenty of sleep? Make sure you continually find times to relax – even if it just for ten minutes at various times throughout the day. This is essential to health.

☐ Get out there on set and get to work. Congratulations! You are now a filmmaker. Now produce your movie. And work to make something awesome! At the same time, have fun!

☐ During production, try to constantly get press to profile your movie. It would be great to create buzz, get people to your website and get them to opt into your newsletter mailing list.

☐ After the WRAP, have a wrap party. Don't sleep with anybody or get drunk or make a fool of yourself! You're a professional. Act like one.

☐ After you recover from your hangover, you will probably start editing the movie. I suggest getting some trusted friends and share the edit suite with another set of eyes.

☐ Your first cut will be rough. Screen it with a group of people who have never seen the movie. Get feedback.

☐ Take the feedback and refine your edit. After that, take a week off – don't look at the movie or play around with it. Then, when you come back to the suite, refine and refine again.

☐ Have a second small screening with people who have never seen the movie. Take notes. Then take those notes back to your edit suite. Then cut the fat.

☐ Add some sound FX to your movie. Clean up actor dialogue and rough areas. Audio is often more important than visual.

☐ Screen the movie again with a new, small set of people. Take notes. Go back and refine.

☐ When you have a cut you're happy with, then you can begin to plan your next strategy. For example, will you go to film festivals? Then you should have a target list in mind.

☐ You may have several opportunities for traditional distribution. With some qualified professionals, analyze the deal. Find out if the deal will fit your business objectives, if not, move on to another next deal.

☐ What if there are no deals? Hopefully you have a strong mailing list, a marketable hook and a plan for reaching your target demographic.

☐ As such, refine your website into a sales funnel hub. Upload your movie to one of the many VOD sites and refine your movie poster and artwork. (To sell your movie via VOD, check out www.MovieSalesTool.com)

☐ Also, upload your trailer to YouTube and all the other video sites on the internet. I prefer to stream from YouTube because I don't have to pay the streaming bandwidth.

☐ Write press releases related to the release of your movie. Have a blog component that details your movie and allows other people to comment.

☐ Conduct key word research and then work keywords and key phrases into your Search Engine Optimization.

☐ Create conversations on website forums related to your type of movie. DO NOT SPAM!

☐ Create both a Facebook and MySpace page for your movie. The purpose of this page is to lead people back to your site.

☐ Have a button on your website so people can click it and instantly tweet about your movie.

☐ In addition to this, if you have the budget, purchase some offline advertising in publications related to your movie.

☐ All of these methods are intended to get people back to your website. The purpose of your site is to get people to watch your movie trailer and click the BUY NOW button. Anything that distracts these visitors must go!

☐ If they do not click, then at least try to get them to opt into your mailing list. For this, utilize www.AudienceList.com

☐ Out of all the people who click the BUY NOW button, many visitors will not buy. But some will actually buy your movie. More targeted traffic helps you sell more units!

☐ Consider utilizing your initial monies to purchase more advertising. If you advertising works, this strategy will allow you to potentially scale up your sales.

☐ Sooner or later, you'll figure out how to jumpstart your next project. And you will realize that making movies and making money making movies is possible.

☐ Tips from the trenches: On average it takes 7 meetings to make a relationship. If you are looking to make things happen, remember this. Persistence without being annoying is key.

☐ One final tip. If you aren't getting rejected every day, you are not working hard enough for your goals.

Sell Your Movie Checklist

☐ Create a website specific to your movie. Go to www.MovieSiteHost.com and grab hosting for your site and reserve your domain name. When you purchase your hosting, a domain name is usually included in the purchase price.

☐ Branding is the marketing equivalent of matching your belt with your shoes. Don't make your marketing complicated. Make sure your colors, logos, posters and fonts are consistent.

☐ Most filmmakers make a crazy website with all sorts of bells and whistles. Your website should be simple. You should have a trailer, an about page, a buy now button, links to your social networks and an audience list.

☐ Out of everything I mention, getting people onto your audience list is most important. An audience list will allow you to collect a name and email address of your visitor. To build an opt-in list, which is FREE for the first 500 subscribers, check out: www.AudienceList.com

☐ Take a moment to think about your target audience. Hopefully you have a marketable hook for your movie, and a plan for reaching your target demographic. If not, figure it out!

☐ Get your movie selling as a Video on Demand rental and download. To do this, upload your movie to the many VOD marketplaces, such as iTunes, Amazon and NetFlix. For an easy way to accomplish this, try www.MovieSalesTool.com

☐ You can sell DVDs too. Amazon's CreateSpace makes this easy. Stay out of the shipping business. Let CS manufacture your DVDs and fulfill your orders on demand.

☐ Your trailer is your sales tool. Upload your trailer to YouTube as well as many other, popular video sites.

☐ Make sure your trailer mentions your website. Put your focus on optimizing YouTube. Why? Because YouTube is both a social network and the second largest search engine on earth (also owned by Google.) It's worth it!

☐ Write press releases related to the availability of your movie. Include back links to your site. Send the release out via one of the online press release submission sites. In addition to this, don't be afraid to call magazine editors and journalists who write for your target audience. As they say, if you don't ask – you don't get!

☐ Join online forums related to your target market. Create a profile, complete with a signature link to your website. Now, whenever you join a conversation, you'll spread your links.

☐ Just because you're in a forum doesn't mean people care about you or your movie. If you join conversations without adding value – or if you become one of those spam happy people who talk about your movie and fail to add value to the discussion, you will be seen as a spammer.

☐ If the idea of contributing to forum conversations annoys you, then just pay for advertising on the site. The whole point is to increase awareness of your movie and get prospective audience members to your site.

☐ Create a Facebook page, a Twitter account and join the popular social networking sites. Again, you'll want to build a fan base for your movie. And to manage it, try www.Ping.Fm This tool allows you to update all your social networking sites at once, which is cool!

☐ The purpose of using social networks is to connect with your target market, spread word about your movie and once again, lead people off the networks and onto your Audience list.

☐ The reason you cannot rely solely on social networking for your audience list, is because many of those sites have gone out of vogue. I lost 10K "friends" on one of them. As a result, I estimate this tip is worth $100,000.00.

☐ Additionally, have your webmaster put a button on your website so people can tweet, bookmark, and share your movie website with friends on their social networking sites. (Can you please click the tweet button at the top of this article?)

☐ If you have the budget, purchase offline advertising in publications related to your movie. To find related publications, go to a bookstore and look for magazines. Also, conduct several Google searches to find influencers in the space.

☐ All of these methods are intended to get people back to your website. The purpose of your site is to get people to watch your movie trailer and click the BUY NOW button. Anything that distracts these visitors must go!

☐ You will soon realize that most people will not buy your movie on their first visit to your website. If they don't click, then at least try to get them to opt into your audience list. Then you have a chance of getting them to buy later.

☐ Out of all the people who click the BUY NOW button, many will not buy. This is totally normal. Your goal is to continually find ways to increase targeted web traffic.

☐ Consider using that money to purchase more advertising and then repeat the cycle. The goal is to keep investing and reinvesting the money until you produce a self-sustaining machine.

☐ Sales will tend to level off after a few years. This is the normal. When this happens, find some other filmmakers with a movie geared towards the same target audience. Offer to promote their movie to your audience list.

☐ If other filmmakers have an audience list, ask them to promote your movie. Be willing to pay them a cut of your profits.

☐ Time for your next project! But unlike before, you'll have a strong mailing list at your disposal. And as a result, you can now ask yourself the following magical questions: "How many VOD downloads do I have to sell to recoup my investment? And how am I going to sell them?" Answer those questions, and you'll also be talking the talk with your investors.

How to Create a Press Kit

Assuming you are like most filmmakers with a movie, you have been building a bunch of relationships on your social networking sites. The next step in the process of filmmaking promotion is designing your press kit.

If you do not hire a publicist, you will need to create your own press kit. It's actually not that difficult. A press kit is basically a bunch of stuff shoved into a neat-o folder that tells people what the heck your movie is about. Maybe I'm over simplifying the process...But it's not too difficult. Here are some things you will want to include:

Cover Sheet: The cover sheet is basically the top sheet that grabs everyone's attention and promotes the hook of the movie. In some ways, it's sort of like a mini-poster that includes the title, contact info, some good quotes from previous reviews, the same cast and crew credits from the poster and mention of any film festival awards you have won.

Synopsis: You should already have a pretty solid synopsis. If you do, just cut and paste it into the press kit. If not, you'll need one. So write it. Some people add action photos from the movie to this page. This is fine, as long as the photos look good.

Photos: Get some journalist friends to check out your production photos. Pick a few that seem incredibly interesting and do a good job of making people want to see the movie. Include them in the kit.

Cast and Crew: This is pretty simple. Just put together some bios of the main cast and crew and include them on the page next to a miniature headshot.

Anecdotes: This is the story of how the film got made. For this, you can write about memorable moments, such as when the camera broke 25 times after traffic delayed the first day of shooting for 13 hours and the lead actor caught fire.

Reviews: If you have any good reviews, include them here.

Credits: This is a page devoted to the full cast and crew credits.

Putting a press kit together is not overly complex. But if you would rather spend your time on higher level tasks, I suggest you go into your network and post the following:

"Low-budget filmmaker seeks publicist to help make a press kit and get the word out about our movie. Will pay $500 upon completion of press kit." Something like this should help.

Acknowledgements

This book represents the first chapter in what continues to be an awesome, filmmaking filled life. So without sounding overly self-important I'd like to thank a few people. Firstly, I thank my mom and dad for being the best parents I ever had.

Brett Schmid provided great insight on women, music, money and life. James Slusser believed in me before I believed in myself. Dr. Dana Uloth coached me through my first film. Geoff Ulloth coached me through my second. Bill Heidlebaugh gave me a job and my first story. Kim Lefever taught me good writing begins with a crappy first draft. Wayne Broderick taught me every frame matters. The entire group at JPL.

Dean Craigo for initial work in NYC. Heather Huzovic for subway navigation, sushi eating and how to hail a taxi. Special thanks goes to my aunt Kim Eberly for allowing me to sleep on her sofa. During that time, Craig Spector always took my calls and provided awesome advice. One profound life and business lesson came from Seth Carmichael, who taught me to NEVER ask permission to make things happen!

Thanks to Jared Tweedie for ongoing friendship.

Then there is Kim Callahan who reminds me to "keep it real." Ian Hannin for endless enthusiasm. Jimmi Simpson reminds me this stuff is possible. Would also thank Melanie Lynskey for encouragement and summer BBQ hospitality. I am constantly amazed by Agi Hirshberg who reminds me to live with purpose. Doctor Bruce Gewertz reminds me that no matter how vast the network, everybody matters. Dana Nugent taught me that small details create the big picture.

Acknowledgements

Then there is Ann Bathavic, Damien Elias and Stacy Salter who provided an opportunity that changed my life...

Terry Brenneman taught me there is black and red in business and black is more fun. I am grateful for his business advice.

Thank you to Nina Jacobson for taking time to sit down and explain the importance of cultivating credibility in this town.

Thanks to Andrew Fierberg, Michael Schiffer, Jerad Anderson, Mr. Barry Primus. Jurgen Wolff, Jon Reiss, Peter D. Marshall, Sheri Candler, Gary King, Gordon Firemark, Tom Malloy, Carole Dean, Norman C. Berns, Von Johnson, Forrest Murray, Elizabeth de Clifford, Douglas Bowers, Nolan Gallagher and Michael Murphy. Richard Abramowitz. Adam Chapnick.

Special thanks to Fred Gleeck for sharing marketing advice.

David Hamilton. Jeanna Pool. Kevin Connell for accountability.

Seth Pollins. Maggie Mahoney. Thomas Socash. Jud Mehring. Joseph Borgiel. Chad Hartman. Sherry Adams. John Witmer. Jessica Geovoni. Phil Bledsoe. Paula Kostick. Lisa Crilly. Thanks to Alexis Gonzalez. Randie Pellegrini. David O'Brien. Manish Segal. Erik Brewer. Jack Giambalvo. Nancy Bolkan. Also, Erik Poole. Carl Storm. Joseph Ort. Kyle R. Guelcher. Sean Simmons. Tim Allison. Gia Bay. Deanna Oerman...

And I thank Joe Surges.

About The Author

Jason Brubaker is a Los Angeles based Independent Motion Picture Producer and an expert in video on demand distribution. He is focused on helping YOU make, market and sell movies more easily by building buzz and creating community around your title.

Jason is a contributing author of The Independent's Guide to Film Distributors, he is the founder of Filmmaking Stuff, a professional resource for independent filmmakers, and his articles on independent movie marketing, distribution and film production have been featured in Movie Maker Magazine.

Brubaker talks about modern distribution to filmmakers around the globe through various filmmaking seminars, film schools, panel discussions and workshops. If you know of any events or film festivals, Jason Brubaker is available for speaking, workshops and panel discussions.

If you would like more information on Jason's speaking topics or availability, please contact:

Info@FilmmakingStuff.com
www.FilmmakingStuff.com/speaking

Made in the USA
Lexington, KY
29 April 2012